双 语 名 著 无 障 碍 阅 读 丛 书

第四级

泰戈尔抒情诗选

Rabindranath Tagore:
An Anthology

［印度］泰戈尔 著

吴岩 译

中 国 出 版 集 团
中 译 出 版 社

图书在版编目（CIP）数据

泰戈尔抒情诗选：英汉对照/（印）泰戈尔著；吴岩译. —北京：中译出版社，2012.7（2017.3重印）

（双语名著无障碍阅读丛书）

ISBN 978-7-5001-3462-6

I. ①泰… II. ①泰… ②吴… III. ①英语—汉语—对照读物 ②抒情诗—作品集—印度—现代 IV. ①H319.4：I

中国版本图书馆CIP数据核字（2012）第149792号

出版发行 / 中译出版社

地　　址 / 北京市西城区车公庄大街甲4号物华大厦六层

电　　话 /（010）68359827；　68359303（发行部）；　53601537（编辑部）

邮　　编 / 100044

传　　真 /（010）68357870

电子邮箱 / book@ctph.com.cn

网　　址 / http://www.ctph.com.cn

出版策划 / 张高里

策划编辑 / 胡晓凯

责任编辑 / 胡晓凯　范祥镇

封面设计 / 潘　峰

排　　版 / 陈　彬

经　　销 / 新华书店

规　　格 / 710毫米×1000毫米　1/16

印　　张 / 12.5

字　　数 / 150千

版　　次 / 2012年7月第一版

印　　次 / 2017年3月第五次

ISBN 978-7-5001-3462-6　　　　　　定价：17.00元

多年以来，中译出版社有限公司（原中国对外翻译出版有限公司）凭借国内一流的翻译和出版实力及资源，精心策划、出版了大批双语读物，在海内外读者中和业界内产生了良好、深远的影响，形成了自己鲜明的出版特色。

二十世纪八九十年代出版的英汉（汉英）对照"一百丛书"，声名远扬，成为一套最权威、最有特色且又实用的双语读物，影响了一代又一代英语学习者和中华传统文化研究者、爱好者；还有"英若诚名剧译丛""中华传统文化精粹丛书""美丽英文书系"，这些优秀的双语读物，有的畅销，有的常销不衰反复再版，有的被选为大学英语阅读教材，受到广大读者的喜爱，获得了良好的社会效益和经济效益。

"双语名著无障碍阅读丛书"是中译专门为中学生和英语学习者精心打造的又一品牌，是一个新的双语读物系列，具有以下特点：

选题创新——该系列图书是国内第一套为中小学生量身打造的双语名著读物，所选篇目均为教育部颁布的语文新课标必读书目，或为中学生以及同等文化水平的社会读者喜闻乐见的世界名著，重新编译为英汉（汉英）对照的双语读本。这些书既给青少年读者提供了成长过程中不可或缺的精神食粮，又让他们领略到原著的精髓和魅力，对他们更好地学习英文大有裨益；同时，丛书中入选的《论语》《茶馆》《家》等汉英对照读物，亦是热爱中国传统文化的中外读者所共知的经典名篇，能使读者充分享受阅读经典的无限乐趣。

无障碍阅读——中学生阅读世界文学名著的原著会遇到很多生词和文化难点。针对这一情况，我们给每一本读物原文中的较难词汇和不易理解之处都加上了注释，在内文的版式设计上也采取英汉（或汉英）对照方式，扫清了学生阅读时的障碍。

优良品质——中译双语读物多年来在读者中享有良好口碑，这得益于作者和出版者对于图书质量的不懈追求。"双语名著无障碍阅读丛书"继承了中译双语读物的优良传统——精选的篇目、优秀的译文、方便实用的注解，秉承着对每一个读者负责的精神，竭力打造精品图书。

愿这套丛书成为广大读者的良师益友，愿读者在英语学习和传统文化学习两方面都取得新的突破。

罗宾德拉纳特·泰戈尔(1861—1941)是印度著名的诗人、小说家、艺术家、社会活动家。于 1861 年 5 月 7 日出生在西孟加拉邦加尔各答市，那是当时英印帝国政治和经济的中心。他的祖父德瓦尔格纳特，以生活豪华而又乐善好施闻名，成了商业时代的"王子"；他的父亲戴温德拉纳特对吠陀和奥义书很有研究，生活简朴纯洁，在社会上被称为"大仙"。

"大仙"生了 14 个子女，罗宾德拉纳特·泰戈尔是他最小的儿子。这小儿子 8 岁时写了他的第一首诗，以后经常在一个笔记本上写些诗句，总要朗诵给长辈们听，"像长出新角的牝鹿，到处用头去碰撞一样。""大仙"喜欢在喜马拉雅山区旅行。罗宾 11 岁时，"大仙"把孩子也带出去走了一趟：白天，高山丛林目不暇给，孩子"总担心，别把那儿的美景遗漏了"，晚上，儿子给父亲唱他所喜欢的颂神曲，父亲给儿子讲天文学。罗宾 14 岁时，在大学杂志《知识幼苗》上发表了第一部叙事诗《野花》，长达 1600 行。便是以喜马拉雅山为背景的。

1878 年，罗宾赴英国学法律，兴致索然，改入伦敦大学学英国文学，并研究西方音乐。1880 年，奉父命中途辍学回家。他对国内外的学校教育都不怎么喜欢，觉得收获不大。他的家庭植根于印度哲学思潮，浸润于印度文学、艺术的传统，又深受西方文化的影响；罗宾主要是在这样的家庭环境的熏陶下自学成才的。1891 年，奉父命下乡管理祖传田产，常泛舟漫游，同佃户有些接触，因而触发了改造农村、"更合理地分配财富"的幻想。为此，1901 年在圣谛尼克坦创办了一所学校(1921 年发展成为"国际大学")。20 世纪初，参加反英的人民运动，以诗歌抨击殖民主义者。他反对暴力，也反对妥协；逐渐与群众运动格格不入时，便退隐了。1913 年获得诺贝尔文学奖。1915 年结识甘地。1919 年发生阿姆利则惨案，泰戈尔愤而放弃英国政府封他的"爵士"称号，从此重新面对现实，关心印度的命运和世界大事。他几次出国，访问过中国、日本、英国、美国、拉美、西欧和苏联，他赞美社会主义的苏联，谴责法西斯主义的猖獗。1941 年 4 月，他写下《文明的危机》，控诉英国在印度的殖民统治，深信祖国必将获得民族独立。同年 8 月 7 日，泰戈尔在加尔各答去世。

泰戈尔多才多艺，一生创作了 50 多部诗集，12 部中、长篇小说，100 多篇短篇小说，20 多个剧本，1500 多幅画，以及大量的歌曲和文学、哲学、政治方面的论著。从总体看来，他首先是个诗人；授予他诺贝尔文学奖，主要是由于他的诗歌创作，特别是《吉檀迦利》。

吴岩

1986 年夏

目 录 CONTENTS

Rabindranath Tagore

Stray Birds

飞鸟集

1

Stray[1] birds of summer come to my window to sing and fly away.

And yellow leaves of autumn, which have no songs, flutter and fall there with a sigh.

4

It is the tears of the earth that keep her smiles in bloom.

8

Her **wistful**[2] face **haunts**[3] my dreams like the rain at night.

9

Once we dreamt that we were strangers.

We wake up to find that we were dear to each other.

25

Man is a born child, his power is the power of growth.

36

The waterfall sings, "I find my song, when I find my freedom."

42

You smiled and talked to me of nothing and I felt that for this I had been waiting long.

一

夏天的离群漂泊的飞鸟，飞到我的窗前鸣啭歌唱，一会儿又飞走了。

而秋天的黄叶无歌可唱，飘飘零零，叹息一声，落在窗前了。

四

大地的泪水，使她的微笑永不凋谢。

八

她那有所思慕的脸，犹如夜间的雨，萦回在我的梦境里。

九

我们一度梦见彼此是陌路人。

醒来时发现我们是相亲相爱的。

二五

人是个天生的孩子，人的力量是生长壮大的力量。

三六

瀑布唱道："我找到了自由，也就找到了歌。"

四二

你微笑，对我默默无言，可我觉得，我为此情此境，已经等待很长久了。

① stray /streɪ/ *a.* 离群的，迷路的

② wistful /'wɪstfʊl/ *a.* 渴望的，思念的

③ haunt /hɔːnt/ *v.* 萦绕在心头

45

He has made his weapons his gods.

When his weapons win he is defeated himself.

46

God finds himself by creating.

55

My day is done, and I am like a boat drawn on the beach, listening to the dance-music of the tide in the evening.

72

In my **solitude**[1] of heart I feel the sigh of this widowed evening **veiled**[2] with mist and rain.

74

The **mist**[3], like love, plays upon the heart of the hills and bring out surprises of beauty.

83

He who wants to do good knocks at the gate; he who loves finds the gate open.

85

The artist is the lover of Nature, therefore he is her slave and her master.

104

The music of the far-away summer flutters around the Autumn seeking its former nest.

四五

他把他的武器当作神明。

他的武器胜利时，他自己也就失败了。

四六

上帝在创造中发现他自己。

五五

我的白昼已经完了，我像是一只拖到了海滩上的小船，静听着黄昏涨潮的舞乐。

七二

这蒙着雾和雨的茕独的黄昏，我在我心的孤寂里，感觉到了它的叹息。

七四

雾，像爱情一样，在山峦的心上游戏，创造出了种种惊人的美丽。

八三

想行善的，叩门；而爱人的，看见门敞开着哩。

八五

艺术家是自然的爱人，因而艺术家既是自然的奴隶，又是自然的主人。

一○四

遥远的夏季的音乐，余音缭绕着秋季，在寻访它的旧巢。

① solitude /ˈsɔlɪtjuːd/ n. 荒野；孤独

② veil /veɪl/ v. 遮盖，掩饰

③ mist /mɪst/ n. 薄雾

106

The touch of the nameless days clings to my heart like mosses round the old tree.

112

The sun has his simple **robe**[①] of light. The clouds are **decked**[②] with **gorgeousness**[③].

120

I feel **thy**[④] beauty, dark night, like that of the loved woman when she has put out the lamp.

122

Dear friend, I feel the silence of your great thoughts of many a deepening **eventide**[⑤] on this beach when I listen to these waves.

126

Not hammer-strokes, but dance of the water sings the pebbles into perfection.

130

If you shut your door to all errors truth will be shut out.

139

Time is the wealth of change, but the clock in its **parody**[⑥] makes it mere change and no wealth.

① robe /rəʊb/ *n.* 睡袍,长袍

② deck /dek/ *v.* 装饰;打扮

③ gorgeous /'gɔːdʒəs/ *a.* 漂亮的,华美的

④ thy /ðaɪ/ *a.* （旧式用法）你的

⑤ eventide /'iːvəntaɪd/ *n.* 黄昏,日暮

⑥ parody /'pærədɪ/ *n.* 滑稽的模仿诗文

一〇六

无名日子的感触，我至今耿耿于怀，正如苍苔黏附在老树周身。

一一二

太阳披着朴素的光明之袍。彩云则衣饰华丽。

一二〇

黑夜，我感觉到你的美了，你美如一个可爱的妇人，才把灯火捻灭。

一二二

亲爱的朋友，多少个暮色深沉的黄昏里，我在这个海滩上谛听着海涛澎湃的时候，我感受到了你那伟大思想的沉默。

一二六

使卵石臻于完美的，并非锤的打击，而是水的且歌且舞。

一三〇

如果你把所有的错误都关在门外，那么，真理也要被排斥了。

一三九

时间是变化的财富，然而时钟拙劣地模仿，却只有变化而毫无财富。

150

My thoughts **shimmer**[①] with these shimmering leaves and my heart sings with the touch of this sunlight; my life is glad to be floating with all things into the blue of space, into the dark of time.

156

The Great walks with the Small without fear.

The Middling keeps **aloof**[②].

176

The water in a **vessel**[③] is **sparkling**[④]; the water in the sea is dark.

The small truth has words that are clear; the great truth has great silence.

181

My flower of the day dropped its petals forgotten.

In the evening it ripens into a golden fruit of memory.

183

The evening sky to me is like a window, and a lighted lamp, and a waiting behind it.

198

The cricket's **chirp**[⑤] and the patter of rain come to me through the dark, like the **rustle**[⑥] of dreams from my past youth.

一五〇

　　我的思想随着闪烁的绿叶闪烁，我的心随着阳光的爱抚歌唱，我的生命乐于随同万物浮游于空间的蔚蓝里，时间的墨黑里。

一五六

　　伟大者，不怕与弱小者同行。

　　中庸者，却远而避之。

一七六

　　杯中的水闪闪生光，海里的水是黑沉沉的。

　　小道理可用文字说清楚；大道理却只有伟大的沉默。

一八一

　　我的白昼之花落下了它那被人遗忘的花瓣。

　　这花在黄昏里便成熟为一颗记忆的金果。

一八三

　　在我看来，黄昏的天空，好比一扇窗子，一盏点亮的灯，灯下的一次等待。

一九八

　　蟋蟀唧唧，夜雨潇潇，透过黑暗传到我的耳边，仿佛我那逝去的青春，衣衫有声地来到我的梦里。

---

① shimmer /'ʃɪmə/ v. 闪闪发光;发微光

② aloof /ə'luːf/ a. 冷淡，疏远的;孤零零的

③ vessel /'vesl/ n. 容器

④ sparkling /'spɑːklɪŋ/ a. 闪烁的,闪闪发光的

⑤ chirp /tʃɜːp/ n. 鸟叫;虫鸣

⑥ rustle /'rʌs(ə)l/ v. 沙沙声,飒飒声

200

The burning log bursts in flame and cries, — "This is my flower, my death."

202

"I cannot keep your waves," says the bank to the river.

"Let me keep your footprints in my heart."

214

Our desire lends the colours of the rainbow to the mere mists and **vapours**[①] of life.

224

My friend, your great heart shone with the sunrise of the East like the snowy summit of a lonely hill in the dawn.

240

Rockets, your insult to the stars follows yourself back to the earth.

243

The stream of truth flows through its channels of mistakes.

249

Dark clouds become heaven's flowers when kissed by light.

255

Find your beauty, my heart, from the world's movement, like the boat that has the grace of the wind and the water.

二〇〇

燃烧着的原木，爆发出火焰，大声叫道："这是
我的花朵，我的死亡。"

二〇二

河岸对河流说："我无法留住你的波涛，
让我把你的足印留在我的心上吧。"

二一四

我们的欲望，把长虹绚烂的色彩，借给了只不过
是云雾的人生。

二二四

我的朋友，你的心正如晨光里孤寂山岭的积雪峰
巅，随着东方日出而放射光芒。

二四〇

爆竹啊，你对繁星的侮辱，跟着你回到了地上。

二四三

川流不息的真理，通过错误的沟渠，奔涌而出。

二四九

乌云受到阳光的接吻，便变成天上的鲜花。

二五五

我的心啊，从世界的运动中探索你的美吧，正如
小舟之美，得之于风与水的激荡。

① vapour /'veɪpə/ *n.* 雾气

266

I do not ask **thee**[1] into the house.

Come into my **infinite**[2] loneliness, my Lover.

267

Death belongs to life as birth does.

The walk is in the raising of the foot as in the laying of it down.

269

The night's flower was late when the morning kissed her, she **shivered**[3] and sighed and dropped to the ground.

272

Let my thoughts come to you, when I am gone, like the afterglow of sunset at the **margin**[4] of starry silence.

279

Let the dead have the **immortality**[5] of fame, but the living the immortality of love.

280

I have seen thee as the half-awakened child sees his mother in the dusk of the dawn and then smiles and sleeps again.

283

Love is life in its fulness like the cup with its wine.

① thee /ðiː/ *pron.* 〈古〉你
② infinite /'ɪnfɪnɪt/ *a.* 无限的,无边无际的

③ shiver /'ʃɪvə/ *v.*（因寒冷,害怕等）颤抖

④ margin /'mɑːdʒɪn/ *n.* 边沿,边缘

⑤ immortality /ɪmɔː'tæləti/ *n.* 不朽；不灭

二六六

我的爱人,我不要求你进我的屋子,

你到我的无穷孤寂里来吧。

二六七

死亡属于生命,正如诞生一样。

走路需要举足,正如需要落足一样。

二六九

黑夜之花开迟了,当晨光吻她的时候,她浑身战栗,唏嘘叹息,终于萎落到地上了。

二七二

当我离去的时候,让我的思想来到你的身边,正如那夕阳的余晖,映在寂静星空的边缘。

二七九

让死者有不朽的名誉,生者有不朽的爱情。

二八○

神啊,我看见了你,就像似醒非醒的孩子,在黎明的薄暗里看见了他的母亲,于是微微一笑又睡去了。

二八三

爱是充实圆满的生命,正如斟满了酒的杯子。

291

Clouds come floating into my life from other days no longer to **shed**[1] rain or **usher**[2] storm but to give colour to my sunset sky.

299

God waits for man to regain his childhood in wisdom.

301

Thy sunshine smiles upon the winter days of my heart, never doubting of its spring flowers.

308

Tonight there is a **stir**[3] among the palm leaves, a **swell**[4] in the sea, Full Moon, like the heart throb of the world. From what unknown sky **hast**[5] **thou**[6] carried in thy silence the aching secret of love?

309

I dream of a star, an island of light, where I shall be born and in the depth of its quickening leisure my life will ripen its works like the rice-field in the autumn sun.

316

Man's history is waiting in patience for the **triumph**[7] of the insulted man.

317

I feel thy gaze upon my heart this moment like the sunny silence of

① shed /ʃed/ v. 流出，流下，洒
② usher /'ʌʃə/ v. 引，领，陪同

③ stir /stə:/ n. 搅动；搅和；搅拌
④ swell /swel/ n. 汹涌
⑤ hast /hæst/ have 的第二人称单数现在式
⑥ thou /ðaʊ/ pron. 你

⑦ triumph /'traɪəmf/ n. 胜利，成功

二九一

从往昔日子里飘浮到我生活里来的云层，再也不降下雨点或引起风暴了，却给我那夕阳返照的天空添上了色彩。

二九九

神等待着人在智慧里重新获得他的童年。

三〇一

您的阳光对我心头的冬日微笑，从不怀疑这心的春华。

三〇八

今夜，棕榈叶子哗啦啦地响，海上涌起大波大浪，仿佛世界在心悸心颤。月亮啊，你从什么不可知的天空里，默默无言地带来了爱情的痛苦秘密呢？

三〇九

我梦见一颗星，一个光明之岛，我将在那儿出生，在它那生气勃勃的闲暇深处，我生命的事业将臻于成熟，仿佛秋天阳光下的稻田。

三一六

人类的历史，耐心地等待着被侮辱者的胜利。

三一七

此刻我感到你的凝视落在我的心上，仿佛早晨阳

the morning upon the lonely field whose harvest is over.

320

I have **scaled**[1] the peak and found no shelter in fame's **bleak**[2] and **barren**[3] height. Lead me, my Guide, before the light fades, into the valley of quiet where life's harvest **mellows**[4] into golden wisdom.

光灿烂的沉默，落在已经收割过的孤寂的田地上。

三二〇

我攀上高峰，发现名誉的高处荒凉贫瘠，找不到栖身之所。我的导师啊，趁着光明尚未消失，领我进入安静的山谷，让一生的收获在山谷里成熟，化为黄金般的智慧。

① scale /skeɪl/ v. 攀登，爬

② bleak /bliːk/ a. 阴冷的；荒凉的

③ barren /'bærən/ a. 贫瘠的

④ mellow /'meləu/ a.（水果）熟透的

Fruit-Gathering

采果集

1

Bid me and I shall gather my fruits to bring them in full baskets into your courtyard, though some are lost and some not ripe.

For the season grows heavy with its fulness, and there is a **plaintive**[1] shepherd's pipe in the shade.

Bid me and I shall set sail on the river.

The March wind is **fretful**[2], fretting the languid waves into murmurs.

The garden has yielded its all, and in the weary hour of evening the call comes from your house on the shore in the sunset.

2

My life when young was like a flower—a flower that loosens a petal or two from her abundance and never feels the loss when the spring breeze comes to beg at her door.

Now at the end of youth my life is like a fruit, having nothing to spare, and waiting to offer herself completely with her full burden of sweetness.

4

I woke and found his letter with the morning.

I do not know what it says, for I cannot read.

I shall leave the wise man alone with his books, I shall not trouble him, for who knows if he can read what the letter says.

Let me hold it to my forehead and press it to my heart.

When the night grows still and stars come out one by one I will

一

吩咐我，我就采集果实，一筐筐装得满满的，送到你的院子里，尽管有的失落了，有的尚未成熟。

由于丰收，季节不胜重负，而绿荫里有凄婉的牧笛声。

吩咐我，我就在河上启碇扬帆。

三月的风是暴躁的，把懒洋洋的水波激荡得潺潺有声。

花园已经献出它的一切果实，在黄昏倦怠的时刻里，从夕阳西下的岸边，从你那所房子里，又传来了呼唤的声音。

二

年轻的时候，我的生命像一朵花——这朵花在和煦春风来到她门口乞求时，从她的丰盛里施舍一两片花瓣，也从不感到什么损失。

如今青春已逝，我的生命像一颗果实，已无他物可施可舍，只等着把果实本身及其所负荷的充盈的甜蜜，完全贡献出来。

四

我醒来，发现他的信与清晨俱来。

我不知道信里说什么，因为我不识字。

且让聪明人径自去读他的书，我不想麻烦他，因为谁知道他能否看懂信里的话。

让我把信举到额上，按在心头。

夜阑人静，繁星一颗颗出现时，我要把信摊在膝上，悄然独坐。

① plaintive /ˈpleɪntɪv/ *a.* (声音)哀怨的,忧郁的

② fretful /ˈfretfʊl/ *a.* 烦躁不安的

spread it on my lap and stay silent.

The rustling leaves will read it aloud to me, the rushing stream will **chant**[①] it, and the seven wise stars will sing it to me from the sky.

I cannot find what I seek, I cannot understand what I would learn; but this unread letter has lightened my burdens and turned my thoughts into songs.

6

Where roads are made I lose my way.

In the wide water, in the blue sky there is no line of a track.

The pathway is hidden by the birds' wings, by the star-fires, by the flowers of the **wayfaring**[②] seasons.

And I ask my heart if its blood carries the wisdom of the unseen way.

15

Your speech is simple, my Master, but not theirs who talk of you.

I understand the voice of your stars and the silence of your trees.

I know that my heart would open like a flower; that my life has filled itself at a hidden fountain.

Your songs, like birds from the lonely land of snow, are **winging**[③] to build their nests in my heart against the warmth of its April, and I am content to wait for the merry season.

18

No: it is not yours to open buds into blossoms.

Shake the bud, strike it; it is beyond your power to make it

① chant /tʃɑ:nt/ v. 反复
地唱（吟咏或说）

绿叶萧萧，会替我朗诵这信；流水汩汩，会替我吟咏这信；而智慧七星会在天空里替我歌唱这信。

我找不到我寻觅的，我不理解我要学习的，可这封未读的信减轻了我的负担，而且把我的思想转化成了歌曲。

六

在铺有道路的地方，我迷了路。

在浩渺大水上，在瓦蓝天空里，没有一丝儿路径的迹象。

② wayfaring /'weɪfeərɪŋ/
a. 旅行的

路径被众鸟的翅膀、天上的星火、四季流转的繁花遮掩了。

于是我问我的心，它的血液里可有智慧能发现那看不见的道路。

十五

你讲的话朴实无华，我的主啊，可那些讲起你的人，他们的话并不如此。

我懂得你的繁星的话语，懂得你的树林的沉默。

我知道我的心会像一朵花儿似的盛开；知道我的生命已经在隐秘的泉水边充实了自己。

③ wing /wɪŋ/ v. 飞

你的歌曲，仿佛来自寂寥雪原的飞鸟，要飞到我心头筑巢，迎迓四月的温暖，而我也满足于等待那欢乐的季节。

十八

不，催蓓蕾开花，你可办不到。

摇撼蓓蕾也好，敲打蓓蕾也好，催它开花你可无能为力。

blossom.

Your touch **soils**[1] it, you tear its petals to pieces and **strew**[2] them in the dust.

But no colours appear, and no perfume.

Ah! it is not for you to open the bud into a blossom.

He who can open the bud does it so simply.

He gives it a glance, and the life-sap stirs through its veins.

At his breath the flower spreads its wings and flutters in the wind.

Colours flush out like heart-longings, the perfume betrays a sweet secret.

He who can open the bud does it so simply.

21

I will meet one day the Life within me, the joy that hides in my life, though the days **perplex**[3] my path with their idle dust.

I have known it in glimpses, and its fitful breath has come upon me, making my thoughts fragrant for a while.

I will meet one day the Joy without me that dwells behind the screen of light—and will stand in the overflowing solitude where all things are seen as by their creator.

27

Sanâtan was telling his beads by the Ganges when a Brahmin in rags came to him and said, "Help me, I am poor!"

"My alms-bowl is all that is my own," said Sanâtan, "I have given away everything I had."

"But my lord Shiva came to me in my dreams," said the Brahmin,

你的抚摸玷污了它，你撕碎它的花瓣，把它们撒在尘土里。

然而，没有色彩，也没有芳香。

啊！催蓓蕾开花，你可办不到。

他能催蓓蕾开花，他轻而易举。

他看它一眼，生命之液便在它血管里流动。

他吹一口气，花儿便展翅随风飞舞。

色彩纷呈，如内心的渴望，芳香又透露了甜蜜的秘密。

他能催蓓蕾开花，他轻而易举。

二一

总有一天，我会遇见我内心的生命，会遇见藏在我生命中的欢乐，尽管岁月以其闲散的尘埃迷糊了我的道路。

我曾在它隐约闪现时认识它，它的气息一阵阵地袭来，使我的思想芳香片刻。

总有一天，我会遇见那留在光明屏幕后面的、无我的欢乐——我会伫立在横溢欲流的寂寞之中，在那儿，世界万物一目了然，犹如造物主看到的一样。

二七

萨那坦在恒河之滨数着念珠祈祷，一个衣衫褴褛的婆罗门来到他面前，说："我穷苦极了，你行行好吧！"

"化缘的碗是我的全部财产，"萨那坦说，"我已经把我所有的一切都施舍出去了。"

① soil /sɔɪl/ *v.* 弄脏

② strew /struː/ *v.* 撒，使散落

③ perplex /pə'pleks/ *v.* 困惑

"and **counselled**① me to come to you."

Sanâtan suddenly remembered he had picked up a stone without price among the pebbles on the river-bank, and thinking that some one might need it hid it in the sands.

He pointed out the spot to the Brahmin, who wondering dug up the stone.

The Brahmin sat on the earth and mused alone till the sun went down behind the trees, and cowherds went home with their cattle.

Then he rose and came slowly to Sanâtan and said, "Master, give me the least **fraction**② of the wealth that **disdains**③ all the wealth of the world."

And he threw the precious stone into the water.

31

"Who among you will take up the duty of feeding the hungry?" Lord Buddha asked his followers when famine **raged**④ at Shravasti.

Ratnâkar, the banker, **hung**⑤ his head and said, "Much more is needed than all my wealth to feed the hungry."

Jaysen, the chief of the King's army, said, "I would gladly give my life's blood, but there is not enough food in my house."

Dharmapâal, who owned broad acres of land, said with a sigh, "The drought demon has sucked my fields dry. I know not how to pay King's dues."

Then rose Supriyâ, the **mendicant**⑥'s daughter.

She bowed to all and meekly said, "I will feed the hungry."

"How!" they cried in surprise. "How can you hope to **fulfil**⑦ that **vow**⑧?"

① counsel /'kaʊnsəl/ v. 忠告,劝告

② fraction /'frækʃən/ n. 小部分

③ disdain /dɪs'deɪn/ v. 鄙视,蔑视

④ rage /reɪdʒ/ v.（疾病等）肆虐

⑤ hang /hæŋ/ v. 垂下

⑥ mendicant /'mendɪkənt/ n. 托钵僧

⑦ fulfil /fʊl'fɪl/ v. 执行;满足,达成

⑧ vow /vaʊ/ n. 誓言

"可是湿婆大神给我托梦,"婆罗门说, "叫我来求你。"

萨那坦突然记起,他在河滩上卵石堆里捡到过一颗无价宝石,想到也许有人需要它,便把它埋藏在沙土里。

萨那坦给婆罗门指出了地点,婆罗门心中诧异,把宝石挖了出来。

婆罗门坐在地上,独自沉思默想,直至太阳落到树木背后,牧童赶着牛群回家。

于是婆罗门站起身来,缓缓地向萨那坦走去,说道:"大师父,给我那么一点儿鄙夷世间一切财富的财富吧。"

他说罢就把那珍贵的宝石扔到水里去了。

三一

舍卫城饥荒严重,佛祖问他的信徒:

"你们中间有谁愿意承担赈济饥民的责任?"

银行家拉特那卡尔垂首答道: "赈济饥民所需的费用,我倾家荡产也远远不够。"

国王的军队司令詹森说: "我甘愿流血牺牲,然而我自己家里粮食也不够吃的。"

广有良田的达摩波尔长叹一声,说道:"旱魃已经把我的田地吮干了。我还不知道怎样向国王缴纳田赋哩。"

于是托钵僧的女儿苏毕利耶站了起来。

她向大家鞠躬施礼,温顺地说道:"我愿意赈济饥民。"

"啊!"他们惊讶地叫了起来。 "你能指望怎样实现你的誓言呢?"

"I am the poorest of you all," said Supriyâ, "that is my strength. I have my **coffer**[1] and my store at each of your houses."

33

When I thought I would mould you, an image from my life for men to worship, I brought my dust and desires and all my coloured **delusions**[2] and dreams.

When I asked you to mould with my life an image from your heart for you to love, you brought your fire and force, and truth, loveliness and peace.

34

"Sire," announced the servant to the King, "the saint Narottam has never **deigned**[3] to enter your royal temple.

"He is singing God's praise under the trees by the open road. The temple is empty of worshippers.

"They flock round him like bees round the white lotus, leaving the golden jar of honey **unheeded**[4]."

The King, **vexed**[5] at heart, went to the spot where Narottam sat on the grass.

He asked him, "Father, why leave my temple of the golden dome and sit on the dust outside to preach God's love?"

"Because God is not there in your temple," said Narottam.

The King frowned and said, "Do you know, twenty millions of gold went to the making of that **marvel**[6] of art, and it was **consecrated**[7] to God with costly **rites**[8]?"

"Yes, I know it," answered Narottam. "It was in that year when

① coffer /ˈkɔfə/ *n.* 保险箱

② delusion /dɪˈluːʒən/ *n.* 欺骗；迷错觉

③ deign /deɪn/ *v.* 屈尊

④ unheeded /ˌʌnˈhiːdɪd/ *a.* 未被注意的，被忽视的

⑤ vexed /vekst/ *a.* 烦恼的；生气的

⑥ marvel /ˈmɑːvəl/ *n.* 奇迹；令人惊奇的事物

⑦ consecrate /ˈkɔnsɪkreɪt/ *v.* 把…奉为神圣

⑧ rite /raɪt/ *n.* 仪式，典礼

"同你们相比，我是最穷的，"苏毕利耶说道，"那正是我的力量所在。我的金库和粮仓就在你们每个人的家里。"

三三

当我想给你塑造一个脱胎于我的生活的形象，让世人膜拜的时候，我带来了我的尘土和欲望，以及我的色彩缤纷的幻想和梦。

当我要求你用我的生活塑造一个酝酿于你的内心的形象，让你去热爱的时候，你带来了你的火与力，以及真理、美丽与和平。

三四

"陛下，"臣仆向国王禀报道："圣徒那卢达摩从未屈尊进入王家神庙。"

"他在大路旁树荫下唱着颂神的歌。神庙里空空如也，没有礼拜的人。"

"人们成群地围在他身边，像蜜蜂围着白莲花，满不在乎地丢下了盛蜜的金樽。"

国王心中恼火，走到那卢达摩坐在青草上的地方。

国王问他："师父，为什么你离开我的金顶神庙，坐在外边儿尘土里宣讲神的爱？"

"因为神不在你的神庙里。"那卢达摩说。

国王皱着眉头说道："你可知道，修建这座艺术奇迹花了两千万金币，还耗费巨资举行了奉献典礼？"

"是的，我知道的，"那卢达摩答道，"就在那一年，成千上万的老百姓，家里的房子被烧毁了，他们

thousands of your people whose houses had been burned stood vainly asking for help at your door.

"And God said, 'The poor creature who can give no shelter to his brothers would build my house! '

"And he took his place with the shelterless under the trees by the road.

"And that golden bubble is empty of all but hot **vapour**① of pride."

The King cried in anger, "Leave my land."

Calmly said the saint, "Yes, **banish**② me where you have banished my God."

37

Upagupta③, the **disciple**④ of Buddha, lay asleep on the dust by the city wall of Mathura.

Lamps were all out, doors were all shut, and stars were all hidden by the **murky**⑤ sky of August.

Whose feet were those tinkling with anklets, touching his breast of a sudden?

He woke up startled, and the light from a woman's lamp struck his forgiving eyes.

It was the dancing girl, starred with jewels, clouded with a pale-blue mantle, drunk with the wine of her youth.

She lowered her lamp and saw the young face, **austerely**⑥ beautiful.

"Forgive me, young **ascetic**⑦," said the woman; "graciously come to my house. The dusty earth is not a fit bed for you."

The ascetic answered, "Woman, go on your way; when the time is ripe I will come to you."

站在你门口求你帮助，而你不为所动。

于是神说：'好一个可怜可哀的东西，他不能给他的兄弟栖身之所，倒为我修建庙宇！'

于是主和无家可归的人民一起待在大路旁树荫下。

而那金泡里，除了骄傲的热气，空荡荡的，一无所有。"

国王怒气冲冲地喝道："滚出我的国境去。"

圣徒镇静地说道："好吧，从你放逐过神的地方把我放逐出去吧。"

三七

佛的弟子优婆鞠多偃卧在马图拉城墙边的尘土上。

家家户户的灯都灭了，门都关上了，繁星都隐没在八月阴暗的天空里了。

是谁的脚镯叮当的纤足，突然之间碰到了他的胸膛？

他惊醒了，一个妇人掌着灯，灯光照耀着他宽容的眼睛。

原来是个舞女，珠光宝气如繁星闪烁，淡蓝衣裳如轻云缭绕，正沉醉于青春焕发的美酒里。

她把灯儿向下移，看见了他年轻的脸：好不庄严英俊。

"原谅我，年轻的苦修者，"妇人说道，"请光临寒舍吧，尽是尘埃的土地，可不是适宜于你睡觉的地方。"

苦修者答道，"妇人，不用费心了，你径自走吧；

① vapour /'veɪpə/ n. 蒸汽

② banish /'bænɪʃ/ v. 放逐，驱逐

③ Upagupta 优婆鞠多，为佛教中付法藏第四祖，异世五师之一

④ disciple /dɪ'saɪpl/ n. 信徒，门徒

⑤ murky /'mɜːkɪ/ a. 阴暗的；昏暗的

⑥ austerely /ɔs'tɪəlɪ/ ad. 肃穆地；质朴地

⑦ ascetic /ə'setɪk/ n. 苦行者；禁欲主义者

Suddenly the black night showed its teeth in a flash of lightning.

The storm growled from the corner of the sky, and the woman trembled in fear.

......

The branches of the wayside trees were aching with blossom.

Gay notes of the flute came floating in the warm spring air from afar.

The citizens had gone to the woods, to the festival of flowers.

From the mid-sky gazed the full moon on the shadows of the silent town.

The young ascetic was walking in the lonely street, while overhead the lovesick **koels**[1] urged from the mango branches their sleepless **plaint**[2].

Upagupta passed through the city gates, and stood at the base of the **rampart**[3].

What woman lay in the shadow of the wall at his feet, struck with the black **pestilence**[4], her body spotted with sores, hurriedly driven away from the town?

The ascetic sat by her side, taking her head on his knees, and **moistened**[5] her lips with water and **smeared**[6] her body with balm.

"Who are you, merciful one?" asked the woman.

"The time, at last, has come to visit you, and I am here," replied the young ascetic.

43

Over the relic of Lord Buddha King Bimbisâr built a shrine, a **salutation**[7] in white marble.

There in the evening would come all the brides and daughters of the

时机成熟，我自会去找你的。"

突然，闪电一亮，黑夜露出了牙齿。

暴风雨在天空一角咆哮，妇人害怕得发抖。

......

道旁树木繁花满枝，不胜重负。

在温暖的春天空气里，从远方飘来了欢乐的笛声。

城里人到森林里去欢度百花节。

圆月在中天凝望着寂静城市的黑影。

年轻的苦修者在冷冷清清的街上踯躅，而头上是害相思病的杜鹃在芒果树的枝头倾诉失眠的烦恼。

优婆鞠多穿过城门，站在护城堤下。

那患着黑死病、遍体斑疮、被匆匆赶出城外、而今倒卧在他脚下城墙阴影里的妇人是谁呢？

苦修者坐在她身边，让她的头枕在他膝上，用水浸润她的嘴唇，替她浑身涂上香膏。

"慈悲的人，你是谁啊？"那妇人问道。

"看望你的时候终于来临了，所以我到你身边来了。"年轻的苦修者答道。

四三

国王频婆娑罗为佛祖的舍利修建了一座佛龛，一份以白色大理石表达的敬意。

黄昏时分，王室所有的新娘和姑娘都来奉献鲜花，

① koel /'kəuəl/ n.（印度）长尾噪鹃

② plaint /pleɪnt/ n. 悲叹，哀叹

③ rampart /'ræmpɑːt/ n. 防御土墙

④ pestilence /'pestɪləns/ n.瘟疫,疫病

⑤ moisten /'mɔɪsn/ v.（使）变得湿润

⑥ smear /smɪə/ v. 胡乱涂抹

⑦ salutation /ˌsæljʊ'teɪʃən/ n. 招呼，致意,致敬

King's house to offer flowers and light lamps.

When the son became king in his time he washed his father's **creed**[1] away with blood, and lit sacrificial fires with its sacred books.

The autumn day was dying. The evening hour of worship was near.

Shrimati, the queen's maid, devoted to Lord Buddha, having bathed in holy water, and decked the golden tray with lamps and fresh white blossoms, silently raised her dark eyes to the queen's face.

The queen shuddered in fear and said, "Do you not know, foolish girl, that death is the **penalty**[2] for whoever brings worship to Buddha's shrine?

"Such is the king's will."

Shrimati bowed to the queen, and turning away from her door came and stood before Amitâ, the newly wed bride of the king's son.

A mirror of **burnished**[3] gold on her lap, the newly wed bride was braiding her dark long **tresses**[4] and painting the red spot of good luck at the parting of her hair.

Her hands trembled when she saw the young maid, and she cried, "What fearful **peril**[5] would you bring me! Leave me this instant."

Princess Shuklâ sat at the window reading her book of romance by the light of the setting sun.

She started when she saw at her door the maid with the sacred offerings.

Her book fell down from her lap, and she whispered in Shrimati's ears, "Rush not to death, daring woman!"

Shrimati walked from door to door. She raised her head and cried, "O women of the king's house, **hasten**[6]!

"The time for our Lord's worship is come!"

点亮灯火。

王子成为国王以后，用鲜血荡涤了父王的信仰，用神圣的佛经点燃起献祭的火光。

秋日将尽。黄昏礼拜的时辰近了。

侍奉王后的宫女稀丽玛蒂，虔诚信奉佛祖的信女，在圣水里沐过浴，在金盘里摆上明灯和洁白鲜花，默默地抬起她黑色的眸子，仰望着王后的脸。

王后悚然战栗，说道："傻丫头，难道你不知道，凡是去佛龛礼拜奉献的，不论是谁，一律处死？"

"这可是国王的圣旨。"

稀丽玛蒂向王后鞠躬施礼，转身离开王后的房门，走过来站在艾米塔——王子的新婚妻子——面前。

膝上放着一面锃亮的金镜，新嫁娘正编着她又黑又长的辫子，并且在头发分开的地方点上吉祥的朱砂。

她看见这年轻宫女的时候，双手发抖，大声喊道："你会给我带来多么可怕的危险！你给我马上走开！"

公主苏克拉坐在窗边，正就着夕阳的光辉读她的传奇故事。

看见宫女捧着供品站在门口，她吓得跳了起来。

她的书从膝上掉了下来，她凑在稀丽玛蒂的耳朵上低声说道："大胆的丫头，别赶去送死！"

稀丽玛蒂挨门挨户地走过去。

她昂首喊道："王室的妇女们，赶快呀！

我们礼拜佛祖的时候到了！"

① creed /kri:d/ *n.* （尤指宗教）信条,教条

② penalty /'penltɪ/ *n.* 惩罚,处罚

③ burnished /'bɜ:nɪʃt/ *a.* 磨光的,擦亮的

④ tress /tres/ *n.* 一绺头发,卷发

⑤ peril /'perɪl/ *n.* 极大危险

⑥ hasten /'heɪsn/ *v.* 催促；赶紧

Some shut their doors in her face and some **reviled**[1] her.

The last gleam of daylight faded from the bronze dome of the palace tower.

Deep shadows settled in street corners: the **bustle**[2] of the city was hushed: the **gong**[3] at the temple of Shiva announced the time of the evening prayer.

In the dark of the autumn evening, deep as a **limpid**[4] lake, stars throbbed with light, when the guards of the palace garden were startled to see through the trees a row of lamps burning at the shrine of Buddha.

They ran with their swords **unsheathed**[5], crying, "Who are you, foolish one, reckless of death?"

"I am Shrimati," replied a sweet voice, "the servant of Lord Buddha."

The next moment her heart's blood coloured the cold marble with its red.

And in the still hour of stars died the light of the last lamp of worship at the foot of the shrine.

53

I have kissed this world with my eyes and my **limbs**[6]; I have **wrapt**[7] it within my heart in numberless folds; I have flooded its days and nights with thoughts till the world and my life have grown one,—and I love my life because I love the light of the sky so enwoven with me.

If to leave this world be as real as to love it—then there must be a meaning in the meeting and the parting of life.

If that love were deceived in death, then the **canker**[8] of this deceit would eat into all things, and the stars would **shrivel**[9] and grow black.

① revile /rɪ'vaɪl/ v. 辱骂，
痛斥

② bustle /'bʌsl/ n. 忙乱，
热闹

③ gong /gɔŋ/ n. 铜锣；盘
形钟

④ limpid /'lɪmpɪd/ a. 清澈
的，透明的

⑤ unsheathed /'ʌn'ʃiːðd/
a. 抽出鞘的，拔出的

⑥ limb /lɪm/ n. 四肢

⑦ wrap /ræp/ v. 裹；覆盖

⑧ canker /'kæŋkə/ n. 溃
疡，溃烂

⑨ shrivel /'ʃrɪvəl/ v. 枯萎，
干枯，皱缩

有人当着她的面关上房门，有人痛骂她。

白昼的最后一道余晖，从王宫塔楼的紫铜圆顶上消失了。

深沉的阴影栖息在街道角落里：城市的喧嚣沉寂了，湿婆神庙里的钟声，宣告晚祷的时刻来临了。

秋天黄昏的幽暗，深沉如平静的湖，繁星在其间闪烁悸动，这时候，御花园的卫兵，透过树木，惊讶地看见佛龛前亮起一行灯光。

卫兵拔剑出鞘，一面飞跑一面叫喊："你是谁，愚蠢的东西，你不怕死吗？"

"我是稀丽玛蒂，"她柔声答道，"佛祖的仆人。"

紧接着，她心头的热血，溅红了冰冷的大理石。

于是，在繁星的岑寂无声里，佛龛前最后一盏礼拜的灯，熄灭了。

五三

我的眼睛和四肢曾抱吻这个世界，我曾密密层层地把它包起来藏在我的心里；我曾以我的思想激荡它的日日夜夜，直至这个世界和我的生命合为一体，——而我爱我的生命，是因为我爱那与我交织在一起的天空的光明。

如果离开这个世界如同爱这个世界一样真实——那么，人生的离合聚散一定大有意义。

如果爱受到死亡的欺骗，那么，这种欺骗的顽症就会腐蚀万物，繁星亦将萎缩而趋于黯淡无光。

54

The Cloud said to me, "I vanish"; the Night said, "I plunge into the fiery dawn."

The Pain said, "I remain in deep silence as his footprint."

"I die into the fulness," said my life to me.

The Earth said, "My lights kiss your thoughts every moment."

"The days pass," Love said, "but I wait for you."

Death said, "I **ply**[①] the boat of your life across the sea."

55

Tulsidas, the poet, was wandering, deep in thought, by the Ganges, in that lonely spot where they burn their dead.

He found a woman sitting at the feet of the corpse of her dead husband, gaily dressed as for a wedding.

She rose as she saw him, bowed to him, and said, "Permit me, Master, with your blessing, to follow my husband to heaven."

"Why such hurry, my daughter?" asked Tulsidas. "Is not this earth also His who made heaven?"

"For heaven I do not long," said the woman. "I want my husband."

Tulsidas smiled and said to her, "Go back to your home, my child. Before the month is over you will find your husband."

The woman went back with glad hope. Tulsidas came to her every day and gave her high thoughts to think, till her heart was filled to the brim with divine love.

When the month was scarcely over, her neighbours came to her, asking, "Woman, have you found your husband?"

五四

云对我说："我消失了。"夜说："我投进了火红的曙光。"

痛苦说："我保持深沉的缄默，一如足印。"

"我在圆满中死去。"我的生命对我说。

大地对我说："我的光明时时刻刻都在亲吻你的思想。"

"岁月流逝，"爱情说，"然而我一直等着你。"

死亡说："我驾着你的生命之船渡过海去。"

五五

诗人杜尔西达斯在恒河之滨寂寞的火葬场上沉思踯躅。

他看到一个妇人坐在她亡故的丈夫的脚旁，衣饰华丽，仿佛要去参加婚礼。

她看见他时，便站起来施礼，说道："大师，请允许我带着你的祝福跟随先夫进入天堂。"

"为什么这样急急忙忙呢，我的女儿?"杜尔西达斯问道，"这人间岂不也是属于创造天堂的上帝的吗?"

"我不向往天堂，"妇人说道，"我要我的丈夫。"

杜尔西达斯微笑着对她说："回到你家里去吧，我的孩子。不出这个月，你就会找到你的丈夫的。"

妇人怀着快乐的希望回家去了。杜尔西达斯每天去看她，教给她崇高的思想，让她思索体会，直到她心里充满了神圣的爱。

一月未尽，她的邻居来看望她，问道："妇人，

---

① ply /plaɪ/ v. 不断使用，努力从事

The widow smiled and said, "I have."

Eagerly they asked, "Where is he?"

"In my heart is my lord, one with me," said the woman.

62

"What is there but the sky, O Sun, that can hold **thine**[1] image?"

"I dream of thee, but to serve thee I can never hope," the **dewdrop**[2] wept and said, "I am too small to take thee unto me, great lord, and my life is all tears."

"I **illumine**[3] the limitless sky, yet I can yield myself up to a tiny drop of dew," thus the Sun said; "I shall become but a sparkle of light and fill you, and your little life will be a laughing **orb**[4]."

63

Not for me is the love that knows no **restraint**[5], but like the **foaming**[6] wine that having burst its vessel in a moment would run to waste.

Send me the love which is cool and pure like your rain that blesses the thirsty earth and fills the homely earthen jars.

Send me the love that would soak down into the centre of being, and from there would spread like the unseen **sap**[7] through the branching tree of life, giving birth to fruits and flowers.

Send me the love that keeps the heart still with the fulness of peace.

64

The sun had set on the western margin of the river among the tangle

你可找到了你的丈夫?"

寡妇微笑答道："我找到了。"

邻居们忙问："他在哪儿?"

"我的丈夫在我心里，同我成为一体。"妇人说。

六二

"太阳啊，除了天空，还有什么能拥抱你的形象?"

"我梦见你，可我不能指望为你效劳，"露珠呜呜咽咽地说道，"伟大的主啊，我那么渺小，无从拥抱你，我的生命全是泪珠。"

"我照亮无垠的天空，然而我也能倾心于一粒小小的露珠，"太阳这样说道，"我要化作一缕闪烁的光芒去充实你，而你小小的生命便会成为一个欢笑的星球。"

六三

我不要漫无节制的爱，它不过像冒着泡沫的酒，转瞬之间就会从杯中溢出，徒然流失。

请赐我以这样的爱，它清凉纯净，像你的雨，造福干渴的大地，注满家用的陶罐。

请赐我以这样的爱，它渗透到生命的核心深处，由此蔓延开来，仿佛看不见的树液，流遍生命之树的丫枝，使它开花结果。

请赐我以这样的爱，它使我的心因充满和平而长保安宁。

六四

太阳沉落在河流西岸枝条虬结的森林里了。

---

① thine /ðaɪn/ *pron.* 你的
② dewdrop /'djuːdrɔp/ *n.* 露珠,露滴
③ illumine /ɪ'ljuːmɪn/ *v.* 照亮;启发
④ orb /ɔrb/ *n.* 球，天体；圆形物
⑤ restraint /rɪs'treɪnt/ *n.* 抑制,遏制
⑥ foaming /'fəumɪŋ/ *a.* 布满泡沫的
⑦ sap /sæp/ *n.* 树液

of the forest.

The hermit boys had brought the cattle home, and sat round the fire to listen to the master, Guatama, when a strange boy came, and greeted him with fruits and flowers, and, bowing low at his feet, spoke in a bird-like voice-"Lord, I have come to thee to be taken into the path of the supreme Truth.

"My name is Satyakâma."

"Blessings be on thy head," said the master.

"Of what clan art thou, my child? It is only fitting for a Brahmin to aspire to the highest wisdom."

"Master," answered the boy, "I know not of what clan I am. I shall go and ask my mother."

Thus saying, Satyakâma took leave, and **wading** [1] across the shallow stream, came back to his mother's hut, which stood at the end of the sandy waste at the edge of the sleeping village.

The lamp burnt dimly in the room, and the mother stood at the door in the dark waiting for her son's return.

She clasped him to her **bosom** [2], kissed him on his hair, and asked him of his errand to the master.

"What is the name of my father, dear mother?" asked the boy.

"It is only fitting for a Brahmin to **aspire** [3] to the highest wisdom, said Lord Guatama to me."

The woman lowered her eyes, and spoke in a whisper.

"In my youth I was poor and had many masters. **Thou** [4] **didst** [5] come to thy mother Jabâlâ's arms, my darling, who had no husband."

The early rays of the sun glistened on the tree-tops of the forest **hermitage** [6].

隐修的孩子们放牧归来，围坐在篝火边静听高塔马大师讲经；这时来了一个陌生的孩子，向大师献上水果和鲜花，一躬到地，直到他的足下，他用小鸟啁啾般的声音说道："大师啊，我上您这儿来，求您带领我走上那至高无上的真理之路。"

"我的名字叫萨蒂雅卡马。"

"愿神赐福于你。"大师说。

"我的孩子，你属于哪个家族？只有婆罗门才配追求至高无上的智慧。"

"大师，"孩子答道，"我不知道我属于什么家族。我要回家问我的母亲。"

萨蒂雅卡马说罢便告辞大师，蹚过浅浅溪流，回到他母亲的茅屋前。茅屋坐落在荒凉沙滩的尽头，沉沉入睡的村子边上。

房间里灯火昏暗，母亲站在门口黑暗中等待儿子归来。

她把儿子搂在怀里，吻他的头发，问他去见大师的结果。

"亲爱的妈妈，我的爸爸叫什么名字？"孩子问道。

"高塔马大师对我说，只有婆罗门才配追求至高无上的智慧。"

妇人垂下眼睛，低声说道：

"我年轻的时候很穷，侍候过许多老爷。我的宝贝，你确实来到你的妈妈贾宝莱的怀抱里，可我没有丈夫。"

朝辉在静修林的树梢上熠熠生光。

弟子们坐在古老的树木下，面对着大师；他们刚沐过晨浴，蓬乱的头发还是湿漉漉的。

① wade /weɪd/ v. 跋涉

② bosom /'buzəm/ n. 胸部,胸

③ aspire /ə'spaɪə/ v. 渴望,追求

④ thou /ðɑu/ pron. 〈古〉你
⑤ didst /dɪdst/ v. 〈古〉do 的第二人称单数过去式

⑥ hermitage /'hɜːmɪtɪdʒ/ n. 隐居处;修道院

The students, with their tangled hair still wet with their morning bath, sat under the ancient tree, before the master.

There came Satyakâma.

He bowed low at the feet of the sage, and stood silent.

"Tell me," the great teacher asked him, "of what clan art thou?"

"My lord," he answered, "I know it not. My mother said when I asked her, 'I had served many masters in my youth, and thou hadst come to thy mother Jabâlâ's arms, who had no husband.'"

There rose a murmur like the angry hum of bees disturbed in their hive; and the students muttered at the shameless **insolence**[1] of that outcast.

Master Guatama rose from his seat, stretched out his arms, took the boy to his bosom, and said, "Best of all Brahmins art thou, my child. Thou hast the noblest heritage of truth."

69

You were in the centre of my heart, therefore when my heart wandered she never found you; you hid yourself from my loves and hopes till the last, for you were always in them.

You were the inmost joy in the play of my youth, and when I was too busy with the play the joy was passed by.

You sang to me in the **ecstasies**[2] of my life and I forgot to sing to you.

70

When you hold your lamp in the sky it throws its light on my face and its shadow falls over you.

When I hold the lamp of love in my heart its light falls on you and I

萨蒂雅卡马来了。

他一躬到地，直到圣人的足下；然后，他默默伫立。

"告诉我，"伟大导师问他，"你属于哪个家族？"

"我的大师，"孩子答道，"我不知道。我问我妈妈时，她说：'我年轻的时候侍候过许多老爷，你确实来到你的妈妈贾宝莱的怀抱里，可我没有丈夫。'"

人群里响起一阵窃窃私语，仿佛蜂房受到骚扰时蜜蜂发出的嗡嗡愤怒声；弟子们对这贱民无耻的傲慢啧有烦言。

高塔马大师从座位上站起身来，伸出双手把孩子揽在怀里，说道："我的孩子，你是婆罗门中最高贵的。你继承了忠诚老实这一最崇高的传统。"

① insolence /ˈɪnsələns/ *n.* 傲慢

六九

你藏在我的心儿中央，因此，我的心儿在外浪游的时候，她从来没有找到你；你自始至终躲开了我的爱情和希望，因为你始终在爱情和希望里。

你是我青春的游戏里在内心藏得最深的欢乐，我过分孜孜于游戏，倒反而放过了欢乐。

在我生命喜极欲狂的时刻，你向我唱歌，而我却忘了向你唱歌。

② ecstasy /ˈekstəsɪ/ *n.* 狂喜

七〇

你把灯举在空中，灯光照在我的脸上，阴影落在你的身上。

我把爱情之灯擎在我的心里，灯光照在你的身上，

am left standing behind in the shadow.

73

The spring with its leaves and flowers has come into my body.

The bees hum there the morning long, and the winds **idly**[1] play with the shadows.

A sweet fountain springs up from the heart of my heart.

My eyes are washed with delight like the dew-bathed morning, and life is **quivering**[2] in all my limbs like the sounding strings of the lute.

Are you wandering alone by the shore of my life, where the tide is in flood, O lover of my endless days?

Are my dreams flitting round you like the moths with their many-coloured wings?

And are those your songs that are **echoing**[3] in the dark eaves of my being?

Who but you can hear the hum of the crowded hours that sounds in my veins to-day, the glad steps that dance in my breast, the clamour of the restless life beating its wings in my body?

86

THANKSGIVING

Those who walk on the path of pride crushing the lowly life under their tread, covering the tender green of the earth with their footprints in blood;

Let them rejoice, and thank **thee**[4], Lord, for the day is theirs.

But I am thankful that my lot lies with the **humble**[5] who suffer and bear the burden of power, and hide their faces and **stifle**[6] their sobs in

我却被抛在后面阴影里站着。

七三

春天携带着绿叶和繁花进入我的躯体。

整个早晨蜜蜂始终在那儿嗡嗡低鸣，而轻风悠闲地和树影游戏。

一股甘美的泉水从我心中喷涌而出。

我的双眼受到喜悦的冲洗，犹如沐浴在露水里的清晨，我的生命在我的四肢里颤动，犹如琉特琴鸣奏的琴弦。

我的无穷岁月的情人啊，你正在我生命的岸边独自踯躅？岸边正在涨潮啊。

我的梦是否像两翼色彩绚烂的飞蛾，正绕着你飞行？

那些在我生命的黑暗洞穴里回响着的，可是你的歌声？

除了你，还有谁能听见今天我血管里繁忙时刻的嗡嗡声，我胸腔里欢乐的舞步声，我身体里永不静止的生命的轰然鼓翼的声音？

八六

感恩

走在傲慢道路上的人们，把卑贱的生命践踏在他们的脚下，他们沾着鲜血的脚印踏遍了大地的嫩翠新绿。

让他们高兴吧；感谢你，主啊，因为日子是属于他们的。

然而，我是满怀感激之情的，因为我与卑贱者共命运，他们吃苦受难，负荷权势的压榨，在黑暗中掩

① idly /ˈaɪdlɪ/ *ad.* 懒惰地

② quiver /ˈkwɪvə/ *v.* 微颤，抖动

③ echo /ˈekəʊ/ *v.* 回响，回荡

④ thee /ðiː/ *pron.* 〈古〉（thou 的宾格）你

⑤ humble /ˈhʌmbl/ *a.* 卑微的

⑥ stifle /ˈstaɪfl/ *v.* 使窒息；抑制

the dark.

For every throb of their pain has pulsed in the secret depth of thy night, and every insult has been gathered into thy great silence. And the morrow is theirs.

O Sun, rise upon the bleeding hearts blossoming in flowers of the morning, and the torchlight **revelry**[1] of pride **shrunken**[2] to ashes.

面饮泣。

　　他们的每一阵剧痛，都在你黑夜的隐秘深处震颤，他们每次受到的侮辱，都汇入你伟大的沉默。而明天是属于他们的。

　　啊，太阳，从流血的颗颗红心上升起来吧，流血的心正开放出黎明的花朵，而傲慢的狂欢火炬已化为灰烬。

① revelry /'revlrɪ / n. 狂欢;欢宴
② shrunken /'ʃrʌŋkən/ a. 皱缩的;缩小的

The Crescent Moon
新月集

THE HOME

I PACED alone on the road across the field while the sunset was hiding its last gold like a **miser**①.

The daylight sank deeper and deeper into the darkness, and the widowed land, whose harvest had been reaped, lay silent.

Suddenly a boy's shrill voice rose into the sky. He **traversed**② the dark unseen, leaving the track of his song across the **hush**③ of the evening.

His village home lay there at the end of the waste land, beyond the sugar-cane field, hidden among the shadows of the banana and the slender **areca**④ palm, the cocoa-nut and the dark green jack-fruit trees.

I stopped for a moment in my lonely way under the starlight, and saw spread before me the darkened earth surrounding with her arms countless homes furnished with **cradles**⑤ and beds, mothers' hearts and evening lamps, and young lives glad with a gladness that knows nothing of its value for the world.

THE BEGINNING

"WHERE have I come from, where did you pick me up?" the baby asked its mother.

She answered half crying, half laughing, and **clasping**⑥ the baby to her breast,— "You were hidden in my heart as its desire, my darling.

You were in the dolls of my childhood's games; and when with clay I made the image of my god every morning, I made and unmade you then.

You were **enshrined**⑦ with our household **deity**⑧, in his **worship**⑨ I

家 庭

我独自在穿过田野的大路上踽踽而行，夕阳正在把它最后的黄金收藏起来，像个悭吝人一般。

白昼愈来愈深地沉没到黑暗里去了；而孤苦无依的大地，地上的庄稼收割殆尽，默默无言地躺在那儿。

一个孩子的尖锐的声音突然响彻云霄。孩子横渡看不见的黑暗，把他歌声的踪迹，留在黄昏的寂静上。

他那乡村的家庭坐落在荒地尽头、甘蔗田外，藏在香蕉树和细长的槟榔树、椰子树和深绿色的木菠萝树的树影里。

我在星光下我那孤寂的路上小立片刻，看到面前伸展着黑沉沉的大地，大地正以她的双臂环抱着不计其数的家庭，这家家户户都有着孩子的摇篮和大人的眠床，母亲的心和黄昏的灯，以及全然不知其欢乐对于世界的价值的、兴高采烈的年轻的人。

开 端

"我是从哪儿来的，你在哪儿把我捡来的？"婴儿问他的母亲道。

母亲把婴儿紧紧抱在怀里，又是哭又是笑地答道：
"我的心肝，你是我藏在我心里的心愿。

你存在于我童年游戏的泥娃娃之间，每天早晨我用泥土塑我的神像，那时我就把你塑了又毁了。

你同我们的家神一起供在神龛里，我礼拜家神时也礼拜了你。

① miser /'maɪzə/ *n.* 守财奴，吝啬鬼

② traverse /'trævəs/ *v.* 横越，穿越

③ hush /hʌʃ/ *n.* 安静，寂静

④ areca /'ærɪkə/ *n.* 槟榔，槟榔树

⑤ cradle /'kreɪdl/ *n.* 摇篮

⑥ clasp /klæsp/ *v.* 紧抱

⑦ enshrine /ɪn'ʃraɪn/ *v.* 作为神龛以保存某物

⑧ deity /'diːɪtɪ/ *n.* 神；女神

⑨ worship /'wɜːʃɪp/ *v.* 崇拜；尊崇

worshipped you.

In all my hopes and my loves, in my life, in the life of my mother you have lived.

In the lap of the deathless Spirit who rules our home you have been nursed for ages.

When in girlhood my heart was opening its **petals**[1], you **hovered**[2] as a **fragrance**[3] about it.

Your **tender**[4] softness bloomed in my youthful **limbs**[5], like a glow in the sky before the sunrise.

Heaven's first darling, twin-born with the morning light, you have floated down the stream of the world's life, and at last you have **stranded**[6] on my heart.

As I gaze on your face, mystery overwhelms me; you who belong to all have become mine.

For fear of losing you I hold you tight to my breast. What magic has **snared**[7] the world's treasure in these **slender**[8] arms of mine?"

THE JUDGE

SAY of him what you please, but I know my child's **failings**[9].

I do not love him because he is good, but because he is my little child.

How should you know how dear he can be when you try to weigh his merits against his faults?

When I must punish him he becomes all the more a part of my being.

When I cause his tears to come my heart weeps with him.

I alone have a right to blame and punish, for he only may **chastise**[10] who loves.

你曾经生活在我的一切希望和爱情里，你曾经生活在我的生命和我母亲的生命里。

你已经在主宰我们家庭的、不灭的精灵的怀抱里养育了好几个世代了。

我是个姑娘的时候，我的心展开了它的花瓣，而你像馥郁香气缭绕在它的周围。

你的温柔娇嫩，像花一般地盛开在我青春焕发的四肢上，仿佛是日出前天空里的霞光。

天堂的第一个心肝宝贝，晨曦的孪生兄弟，你在世界的生命之流里顺流而下，终于留在我的心头了。

当我端详着你的时候，神秘奥妙之感把我压倒了；原是属于大家的你，竟变成是我的了。

我生怕失掉你，把你紧紧抱在怀里。是什么魔法，使你这世界的珍宝，落到了我纤细手臂的怀抱里？"

裁　判

你爱怎么说他就怎么说吧，可是我倒知道我孩子的弱点的。

我爱他，并不因为他好，而是因为他是我的幼稚的孩子。

权衡他的优点和缺点时，你怎么会知道他有多么可爱？

当我非惩罚他不可的时候，他就变得越发是我的一部分了。

当我使他流泪的时候，我的心和他一同哭泣。

唯独我一个人有权利骂他罚他，因为只有爱他的人才能治他。

① petal /'petl/ n. 花瓣
② hover /'hɔvə/ v. 踌躇，彷徨
③ fragrance /'freɪɡrəns/ n. 芳香,香味
④ tender /'tendə/ a. 娇嫩的
⑤ limb /lɪm/ n. 四肢
⑥ strand /strænd/ v. 搁浅;滞留
⑦ snare /'sneə/ v.（用陷阱、罗网等)捕捉
⑧ slender /'slendə/ a. 苗条的;纤细的
⑨ failing /'feɪlɪŋ/ 缺点，弱点
⑩ chastise /tʃæs'taɪz/ v. 严惩

PLAYTHINGS

CHILD, how happy you are sitting in the dust, playing with a broken **twig**[1] all the morning.

I smile at your play with that little bit of a broken twig.

I am busy with my accounts, adding up figures by the hour.

Perhaps you glance at me and think, "What a stupid game to spoil your morning with!"

Child, I have forgotten the art of being absorbed in sticks and mud-pies.

I seek out **costly**[2] playthings, and gather lumps of gold and silver.

With whatever you find you create your glad games, I spend both my time and my strength over things I never can obtain.

In my **frail**[3] **canoe**[4] I struggle to cross the sea of desire, and forget that I too am playing a game.

THE CHAMPA FLOWER

SUPPOSING I became a champa flower, just for fun, and grew on a branch high up that tree, and shook in the wind with laughter and danced upon the newly **budded**[5] leaves, would you know me, mother?

You would call, "Baby, where are you?" and I should laugh to myself and keep quite quiet.

I should **slyly**[6] open my petals and watch you at your work.

When after your bath, with wet hair spread on your shoulders, you walked through the shadow of the champa tree to the little court where you say your **prayers**[7], you would notice the **scent**[8] of the flower, but

玩　具

孩子，你多么快乐，整个儿早晨坐在泥土里，玩着一根折下来的树枝。

我莞尔微笑，看你玩着那折下来的小小树枝。

我忙于算账，一小时又一小时地把数字加起来，加起来。

也许你瞧我一眼，心中想道："好一个愚蠢的游戏，把你的早晨都糟蹋掉了！"

孩子，聚精会神玩树枝与泥饼的技艺，我已经忘记了。

我搜求昂贵的玩具，收集金块和银块。

你不论找到什么都可以创造出快乐的游戏，我却在我永远得不到的东西上浪费我的时间和精力。

我挣扎着驾驶脆弱的独木舟横渡欲望之海，却忘记了我也在做着游戏。

金香木花

如果我闹着玩儿，变成一朵金香木花，长在那树的高枝上，在风中笑得摇摇摆摆，在新生嫩叶上跳舞，妈妈，你认得出是我吗？

你会叫唤："孩子，你在哪儿啊？"我要暗自好笑，一声也不吭。

我要暗暗展开花瓣，看着你工作。

你洗澡之后，湿发披在两肩，穿过金香木花的阴影，走到小院子里去祈祷时，你会闻到花香芬芳，可

① twig /twɪg/ n. 细枝,嫩枝

② costly /'kɒstlɪ/ a. 昂贵的,贵重的

③ frail /freɪl/ a. 脆弱的,薄弱的

④ canoe /kə'nuː/ n. 小而轻的舟;独木舟

⑤ budded /bʌdɪd/ 发了芽的,有蓓蕾的

⑥ slyly /'slaɪlɪ/ ad. 狡猾地,诡诈地

⑦ prayer /preə/ n. 祈祷,祈祷文

⑧ scent /sent/ n. 气味,香味

not know that it came from me.

When after the midday meal you sat at the window reading Ramayana, and the tree's shadow fell over your hair and your lap, I should fling my **wee**[1] little shadow on to the page of your book, just where you were reading.

But would you guess that it was the tiny shadow of your little child?

When in the evening you went to the cow-shed with the lighted lamp in your hand, I should suddenly drop on to the earth again and be your own baby once more, and beg you to tell me a story.

"Where have you been, you naughty child?"

"I won't tell you, mother." That's what you and I would say then.

FAIRYLAND

IF people came to know where my king's palace is, it would **vanish**[2] into the air.

The walls are of white silver and the roof of shining gold.

The queen lives in a palace with seven courtyards, and she wears a jewel that cost all the wealth of seven kingdoms.

But let me tell you, mother, in a whisper, where my king's palace is.

It is at the corner of our **terrace**[3] where the pot of the tulsi plant stands.

The princess lies sleeping on the far-away shore of the seven impassable seas.

There is none in the world who can find her but myself.

She has **bracelets**[4] on her arms and **pearl**[5] drops in her ears; her

你不知道这芳香是从我身上发出来的。

午餐之后，你坐在窗边读《罗摩衍那》，树影落在你的头发与膝头上时，我要把我小而又小的影子投在你的书页上，就投在你正在阅读的地方。

可你会猜到这就是你的小孩子的小而又小的影子吗？

黄昏时分，你手中掌着点亮的灯，走到牛棚里去，我要突然再落到地上，重新成为你自己的孩子，求你给我讲个故事。

"你这顽皮孩子，你上哪儿去了？"

"妈妈，我才不告诉你呢。"这就是我同你要说的话了。

小小仙境

如果人们知道了我的国王的王宫在什么地方，王宫就会消失在空气里。

宫墙是白色的银子做的，屋顶是闪光的金子做的。

王后住在有七个庭院的御苑里，她佩戴的珠宝，价值七个王国的全部财富。

不过，让我悄悄告诉你，妈妈，我的国王的王宫在什么地方。

王宫就在我们的阳台角落里，安置那盆杜尔茜花的地方。

公主躺在隔着七个不可逾越的海洋的彼岸，沉沉睡去。

除了我自己，世界上没有人能找到公主。

公主手臂上戴着手镯，耳朵上挂着珍珠耳坠，她的长发下垂，拂在地板上。

① wee /wiː/ *a.* 小的，很小的，极小的

② vanish /'vænɪʃ/ *v.* 消失，突然不见

③ terrace /'terəs/ *n.* 台地，梯田

④ bracelet /'breɪslɪt/ *n.* 手镯，臂镯

⑤ pearl /pɜːl/ *n.* 珍珠

hair sweeps down upon the floor.

She will wake when I touch her with my magic wand, and jewels will fall from her lips when she smiles.

But let me whisper in your ear, mother; she is there in the corner of our terrace where the pot of the tulsi plant stands.

When it is time for you to go to the river for your bath, step up to that terrace on the roof.

I sit in the corner where the shadows of the walls meet together.

Only puss is allowed to come with me, for she knows where the **barber**[1] in the story lives.

But let me whisper, mother, in your ear where the barber in the story lives.

It is at the corner of the terrace where the pot of the tulsi plant stands.

THE LAND OF THE EXILE

MOTHER, the light has grown grey in the sky; I do not know what the time is.

There is no fun in my play, so I have come to you. It is Saturday, our holiday.

Leave off your work, mother; sit here by the window and tell me where the desert of Tepântar in the fairy tale is?

The shadow of the rains has covered the day from end to end.

The **fierce**[2] lightning is scratching the sky with its nails.

When the clouds **rumble**[3] and it thunders, I love to be afraid in my heart and cling to you.

When the heavy rain **patters**[4] for hours on the bamboo leaves, and

我用魔杖触动她时，她会醒过来；而她微笑时，珠宝会从她的唇边落下来。

不过，让我凑着你的耳朵悄悄告诉你，妈妈，她就在我们的阳台角落里，安置那盆杜尔茜花的地方。

你要到河边去洗澡的时候，你走到屋顶阳台上来吧。

我就坐在墙垣的影子聚首相会的那个角落里。

我只让小猫咪跟着我，因为小猫咪知道故事里的理发匠住在什么地方。

不过，让我凑着你的耳朵悄悄告诉你，妈妈，故事里的理发匠住在什么地方。

就住在我们的阳台角落里，安置那盆杜尔茜花的地方。

流放的地方

妈妈，天空里的光芒逐渐暗淡；我不知道是什么时候了。

我的游戏一点儿也不好玩，所以我到你身边来了。今天是星期六，是我和你的假日。

放下你的活计吧，妈妈；坐在靠窗的这一边，告诉我，神话里的特潘塔沙漠，究竟在什么地方。

大雨的阴影遮盖着白昼，从这头遮到那头。

凶猛的闪电正在用它的爪子抓着天空。

乌云轰响、雷声隆隆的时候，我心里害怕，我依附在你的身边，我喜欢这样。

① barber /'bɑːbə/ *n.* 理发师

② fierce /fɪəs/ *a.* 强烈的

③ rumble /'rʌmbəl/ *v.* 发出隆隆声

④ patter /'pætə/ *v.* 急速的轻轻拍打

our windows shake and **rattle**[1] at the gusts of wind, I like to sit alone in the room, mother, with you, and hear you talk about the desert of Tepântar in the fairy tale.

Where is it, mother, on the shore of what sea, at the foot of what hills, in the kingdom of what king?

There are no hedges there to mark the fields, no footpath across it by which the villagers reach their village in the evening, or the woman who gathers dry sticks in the forest can bring her load to the market. With **patches**[2] of yellow grass in the sand and only one tree where the pair of wise old birds have their nest, lies the desert of Tepântar.

I can imagine how, on just such a cloudy day, the young son of the king is riding alone on a grey horse through the desert, in search of the princess who lies imprisoned in the giant's palace across that unknown water.

When the **haze**[3] of the rain comes down in the distant sky, and lightning starts up like a sudden fit of pain, does he remember his unhappy mother, abandoned by the king, sweeping the cow-stall and wiping her eyes, while he rides through the desert of Tepântar in the fairy tale?

See, mother, it is almost dark before the day is over, and there are no travellers **yonder**[4] on the village road.

The **shepherd**[5] boy has gone home early from the **pasture**[6], and men have left their fields to sit on mats under the eaves of their huts, watching the **scowling**[7] clouds.

Mother, I have left all my books on the shelf—do not ask me to do my lessons now.

When I grow up and am big like my father, I shall learn all that

① rattle /'rætl/ *v.* 迅速而嘎嘎作响

② patch /pætʃ/ *n.* 小块，小片

③ haze /heɪz/ *n.* 雾霭,烟雾

④ yonder /'jɒndə/ *ad.* 在那边,在远处

⑤ shepherd /'ʃepəd/ *n.* 牧羊人

⑥ pasture /'pæstʃə/ *n.* 牧草地,牧场

⑦ scowl /skaʊl/ *v.* 显得阴沉;威胁

大雨在竹叶上哗啦啦地响上好几个钟点，我家的窗子也随着阵风震得格格地响，这时候，妈妈，我喜欢单独和你一起坐在房间里，听你讲到神话里的特潘塔沙漠。

妈妈，沙漠究竟在哪儿，在什么海的海滩上，在什么山的山麓下，在什么国王的王国里？

那儿没有标明田地疆界的篱笆，也没有村民们可以在晚间走回村子去的，或者妇女们在森林里捡了枯枝可以运到市场上去的小径。特潘塔沙漠躺在那儿，沙土里只有小块的黄色枯草，只有一棵树，一对聪明的老鸟在树上作巢。

我可以想象，就在这样一个乌云满天的日子，国王的年轻的儿子，怎样独自骑着灰色马穿过沙漠，去寻找那被囚禁在不可知的海洋彼岸巨人宫里的公主。

当蒙蒙雨雾从遥远的天空下降，电光闪射如突然发作的疼痛，他可记得他那被国王抛弃的不幸母亲，正在打扫牛棚，擦着眼泪，而他正骑马穿过神话里的特潘塔沙漠？

妈妈，你瞧，白昼还没有完，天色就差不多黑了，那边儿村子里路上已经没有行人了。

牧童早已从牧场上回家来了，人们离开了耕地，坐在屋檐下的草席上，望着那苦着脸的愁云。

妈妈，我把我所有的书都放在书架上了——现在可不要叫我做功课。

等我长大了，长得跟爸爸一样大了，我会把必须

must be learnt.

But just for to-day, tell me, mother, where the desert of Tepântar in the fairy tale is?

PAPER BOATS

DAY by day I float my paper boats one by one down the running stream.

In big black letters I write my name on them and the name of the village where I live.

I hope that someone in some strange land will find them and know who I am.

I load my little boats with shiuli flowers from our garden, and hope that these blooms of the dawn will be carried safely to land in the night.

I **launch**[1] my paper boats and look up into the sky and see the little clouds setting their white bulging sails.

I know not what playmate of mine in the sky sends them down the air to race with my boats!

When night comes I bury my face in my arms and dream that my paper boats float on and on under the midnight stars.

The fairies of sleep are sailing in them, and the **lading**[2] is their baskets full of dreams.

THE FURTHER BANK

I LONG to go over there to the further bank of the river,

Where those boats are tied to the bamboo poles in a line;

Where men cross over in their boats in the morning with **ploughs**[3] on their shoulders to till their far-away fields;

学习的都学到手的。

可是，妈妈，你今天得告诉我，神话里的特潘塔沙漠在哪儿？

纸　船

一天又一天，我把纸船一个个地放在奔流的小河里。

我用又大又黑的字母，在纸船上写下我的名字和我居住的乡村。

我希望在一块陌生的土地上会有人发现这些纸船，知道我是谁。

我从我的花园里采集了秀丽花，装在我的小船里，希望这些曙光之花会安全抵达夜的国土。

我送我的纸船下水，仰望天空，我看到小小云朵正张着鼓鼓的白帆。

我不知道是天空里我的什么游伴，把它们放下来同我的纸船竞赛！

夜来了，我的脸埋在手臂里，我梦见我的纸船在子夜星光下向前漂浮，漂浮。

睡眠的精灵在纸船里扬帆前进，船里载的是装满了梦的篮子。

对　岸

我渴望着要到河对岸去，

那儿的船只排成一行，系在竹竿上，

人们在早晨乘船渡过河去，肩上扛着犁，去耕耘他们的遥远的田地；

① launch /lɔːntʃ/ *v.* 使（船）下水

② lading /leɪdɪŋ/ *n.* 船货，货物

③ plough /plaʊ/ *n.* 犁

Where the **cowherds**[1] make their **lowing**[2] **cattle**[3] swim across to the riverside pasture;

Whence they all come back home in the evening, leaving the **jackals**[4] to **howl**[5] in the island overgrown with weeds,

Mother, if you don't mind, I should like to become the boatman of the ferry when I am grown up.

They say there are strange pools hidden behind that high bank,

Where flocks of wild ducks come when the rains are over, and thick reeds grow round the **margins**[6] where waterbirds lay their eggs;

Where **snipes**[7] with their dancing tails stamp their tiny footprints upon the clean soft mud;

Where in the evening the tall grasses **crested**[8] with white flowers invite the moonbeam to float upon their waves.

Mother, if you don't mind, I should like to become the boatman of the ferryboat when I am grown up.

I shall cross and cross back from bank to bank, and all the boys and girls of the village will wonder at me while they are bathing.

When the sun climbs the mid sky and morning wears on to noon, I shall come running to you, saying, "Mother, I am hungry!"

When the day is done and the shadows **cower**[9] under the trees, I shall come back in the dusk.

I shall never go away from you into the town to work like father.

Mother, if you don't mind, I should like to become the boatman of the ferryboat when I am grown up.

THE FLOWER-SCHOOL

WHEN storm clouds rumble in the sky and June showers come

① cowherd /'kaʊhəːd/ *n.*
牧牛者

② low /ləʊ/ *v.* 哞哞叫

③ cattle /'kætl/ *n.*（总称）
牛；牲口

④ jackal /'dʒækəl/ *n.* 豺

⑤ howl /haʊl/ *v.* 嗥叫

⑥ margin /'maːdʒɪn/ *n.* 边，
边缘

⑦ snipe /snaɪp/ *n.* 鹬

⑧ crested /'krestɪd/ *v.* 被
遮蔽，有障碍

⑨ cower /'kaʊə/ *v.* 蜷缩，
抖缩

牧人们驱赶着哞哞鸣叫的牛群游到对面河边的牧场上去；

黄昏时分，他们都从那儿回家来了，留下豺狼在长满野草的岛上嗥叫。

妈妈，如果你不反对，我长大后要做个摆渡的船夫。

据说，在那高高的河岸背后，藏着许多奇怪的池塘，

下过雨后，便有一群群野鸭来到池上；而环绕池边密密地长着芦苇的地方，水鸟在那儿下蛋；

舞弄着尾巴的沙锥鸟，把它们细小的足印踩在洁净的软泥上；

黄昏时分，头顶着白花的长长茂草，邀请月光在草浪上浮游。

妈妈，如果你不反对，我长大后要做个摆渡的船夫。

我要在两岸之间来来往往，村子里所有在河中洗澡的少男少女都会惊奇地瞧着我。

当太阳爬上中天，早晨变为正午，我要跑到你身边来，说："妈妈，我肚子饿了！"

当白昼完结、阴影在树下哆嗦，我就在暮色中回来。

我决不像爸爸那样离开你到城里去工作。

妈妈，如果你不反对，我长大后要做个摆渡的船夫。

花儿学校

雷电交作的风云在天空隆隆地响，六月的阵雨哗

down,

The **moist**[1] east wind comes marching over the heath to blow its **bagpipes**[2] among the bamboos.

Then crowds of flowers come out of a sudden, from nobody knows where, and dance upon the grass in wild **glee**[3].

Mother, I really think the flowers go to school underground.

They do their lessons with doors shut, and if they want to come out to play before it is time, their master makes them stand in a corner.

When the rains come they have their holidays.

Branches clash together in the forest, and the leaves **rustle**[4] in the wild wind, the thunder-clouds clap their giant hands and the flower children rush out in dresses of pink and yellow and white.

Do you know, mother, their home is in the sky, where the stars are.

Haven't you seen how eager they are to get there? Don't you know why they are in such a hurry?

Of course, I can guess to whom they raise their arms: they have their mother as I have my own.

SYMPATHY

IF I were only a little puppy, not your baby, mother dear, would you say "no" to me if I tried to eat from your dish?

Would you drive me off, saying to me, "Get away, you naughty little puppy?"

Then go, mother, go! I will never come to you when you call me, and never let you feed me any more.

啦啦地倾泻而下，

　　湿潮的东风疾卷过荒原，到竹林里来吹它的风笛，

　　这时，成群的花儿便从谁也不知道的地方冒了出来，欢快地在青草上跳舞。

　　妈妈，我真的觉得花儿们是在地下学校里上学。

　　它们关起校门做功课，如果它们违反校规，过早地跑出来玩儿，它们的老师就要罚它们站在墙角里。

　　大雨来时，花儿们便放假了。

　　树枝在林中磕磕碰碰的，树叶在狂风中簌簌作响，雷电交作的黑云鼓着巨掌，而花儿娃娃们便穿着粉红、鹅黄、雪白的衣裳，冲出来了。

　　妈妈，你可知道，花儿的家是在天上，在星星居住的地方。

　　你没看见花儿们急着要到天上去吗？难道你不知道它们为什么这样急急忙忙吗？

　　当然啦，我猜得出花儿们向谁伸出了双臂：因为花儿自有花儿的妈妈，就像我有我自己的妈妈一样。

同　情

　　如果我不是你的小孩，而只是一只小狗，亲爱的妈妈，我想吃你盘子里的食物时，你会对我说声"不"吗？

　　你会撵我走，对我说，"走开，你这顽皮的小狗"吗？

　　如果这样，那我就走了，妈妈，走了！你叫唤我时，我就决不到你身边来，决不让你再来喂我吃东西了。

---

① moist /mɔɪst/ *a.* 潮湿的，湿润的

② bagpipe /'bægpaɪp/ *n.* 风笛

③ glee /gliː/ *n.* 三部或四部重唱的歌曲

④ rustle /'rʌsl/ *v.* 发出沙沙的声音

If I were only a little green parrot, and not your baby, mother dear, would you keep me chained lest I should fly away?

Would you shake your finger at me and say, "What an ungrateful **wretch**[1] of a bird! It is **gnawing**[2] at its chain day and night?"

Then, go, mother, go! I will run away into the woods; I will never let you take me in your arms again.

VOCATION

WHEN the gong sounds ten in the morning and I walk to school by our lane,

Every day I meet the **hawker**[3] crying, "Bangles, crystal bangles! "

There is nothing to hurry him on, there is no road he must take, no place he must go to, no time when he must come home.

I wish I were a hawker, spending my day in the road, crying, "Bangles, crystal bangles!"

When at four in the afternoon I come back from the school,

I can see through the gate of that house the gardener digging the ground.

He does what he likes with his **spade**[4], he soils his clothes with dust, nobody takes him to task if he gets baked in the sun or gets wet.

I wish I were a gardener digging away at the garden with nobody to stop me from digging.

Just as it gets dark in the evening and my mother sends me to bed,

I can see through my open window the watchman walking up and down.

The lane is dark and lonely, and the street-lamp stands like a giant with one red eye in its head.

如果我不是你的小孩，而只是一只绿色小鹦鹉，亲爱的妈妈，你会用链子把我缚住，生怕我飞走吗？

你会对我指指点点地说："好一只不知感恩的鸟！它日日夜夜咬着链子吗？"

如果这样，那我就走了，妈妈，走了！我就一定逃到森林里去，我就决不让你再把我抱在怀里了。

职　业

早晨，钟敲十下的时候，我穿过小巷上学去。

每天我都遇见小贩在叫卖："镯子啊，亮晶晶的镯子！"

他没有什么急事要办，没有什么路非走不可，没有什么地方非去不可，没有一定的时间非回家不可。

我但愿我也是个小贩，在街道上消磨日子，叫卖着"镯子啊，亮晶晶的镯子！"

下午四点，我放学回家。

我从那所房子的大门口可以望见园丁在掘地。

他拿着铁锹，爱怎么掘就怎么掘，尘土把衣服都弄脏了；如果他在太阳下烤或是被雨水淋湿了，也没有人责备他。

我但愿是个园丁，在花园里一味掘地，根本没有人阻止我。

晚间天色刚黑，我的母亲就送我上床睡觉。

从打开的窗口，我可以看见守夜的更夫走来走去，走去走来。

小巷里黑暗而冷清，路灯站在那儿，像个只生一

① wretch /retʃ/ n. 不幸的人；恶棍
② gnaw /nɔː/ v. 咬，啃
③ hawker /'hɔːkə/ n. 叫卖小贩
④ spade /speɪd/ n. 铁锹

The watchman swings his lantern and walks with his shadow at his side, and never once goes to bed in his life.

I wish I were a watchman walking the streets all night, chasing the shadows with my lantern.

TWELVE O'CLOCK

MOTHER, I do want to **leave off**[①] my lessons now. I have been at my book all the morning.

You say it is only twelve o'clock. Suppose it isn't any later; can't you ever think it is afternoon when it is only twelve o'clock?

I can easily imagine now that the sun has reached the edge of that rice-field, and the old fisher-woman is gathering herbs for her supper by the side of the pond.

I can just shut my eyes and think that the shadows are growing darker under the madar tree, and the water in the pond looks shiny black.

If twelve o'clock can come in the night, why can't the night come when it is twelve o'clock?

AUTHORSHIP

YOU say that father writes a lot of books, but what he writes I don't understand.

He was reading to you all the evening, but could you really make out what he meant?

What nice stories, mother, you can tell us! Why can't father write like that, I wonder?

Did he never hear from his own mother stories of giants and fairies

只红眼睛的巨人。

守夜的更夫提着摇摇晃晃的灯，同他身边的影子一起走动，他生平从来不上床睡觉。

但愿我是个守夜的更夫，整夜在街上走来走去，提了灯追逐着影子。

① leave off 停止，中断

十二点钟

妈妈，我现在真不想做功课了。我整个儿上午都在读书用功。

你说，还不过是十二点钟。就算再晚也晚不过十二点吧；难道你不能把不过十二点钟想象成午后吗？

我能轻易地想象：现在太阳已经落到了稻田边缘，老渔婆正在池塘边采撷香草做她的晚餐。

我只要一闭上眼睛，就能想象到牛角瓜树下的阴影愈来愈黑了，池塘里的水鸟黑发亮。

如果十二点钟能在黑夜里来临，为什么黑夜不能在十二点钟时来临？

写　作

你说爸爸写了许多书，我可不懂得他所写的东西。

他整个儿黄昏都在读书给你听，可你真的能听懂他的意思吗？

妈妈，你能讲给我们听多么美妙动听的故事！我弄不明白，为什么爸爸不能这样写书？

难道他从来没有从他自己的妈妈那儿听到过关于巨人、神仙和公主的故事吗？

and princesses?

Has he forgotten them all?

Often when he gets late for his bath you have to go and call him a hundred times.

You wait and keep his dishes warm for him, but he goes on writing and forgets.

Father always plays at making books.

If ever I go to play in father's room, you come and call me, "what a naughty child! "

If I make the slightest noise, you say, "Don't you see that father's at his work?"

What's the fun of always writing and writing?

When I take up father's pen or pencil and write upon his book just as he does,—a, b, c, d, e, f, g, h, i,—why do you **get cross with**[1] me, then, mother?

You never say a word when father writes.

When my father wastes such heaps of paper, mother, you don't seem to mind at all.

But if I take only one sheet to make a boat with, you say, "Child, how troublesome you are! "

What do you think of father's spoiling sheets and sheets of paper with black marks all over on both sides?

THE WICKED POSTMAN

WHY do you sit there on the floor so quiet and silent, tell me, mother dear?

The rain is coming in through the open window, making you all

他已经完全忘了吗?

爸爸时常拖拖拉拉,耽误了洗澡,你不得不上百次地催他。

你等候着,你替他把菜肴温着,可他一个劲儿写下去,忘记吃了。

爸爸始终玩着写书的游戏。

如果我闯到爸爸的房间里去玩耍,你就要来叫我,说我是"一个多么淘气的孩子!"

如果我稍微出点儿声音,你就会说:"难道你没看见你爸爸在工作吗?"

老是写呀写呀的,又有什么趣味呢?

当我拿起爸爸的钢笔或铅笔,在他的书上像他那样的写字:a, b, c, d, e, f, g, h, i——那时你又为什么跟我生气,妈妈?

爸爸写字的时候,你可从来不说一句话的。

我爸爸浪费掉那么大堆大堆的纸,妈妈,你好像都满不在乎。

可是,我不过拿一张纸折了一只船,你就会说:"孩子,你真烦人!"

爸爸把一张又一张的纸头,正反两面都用密密麻麻的黑色记号糟蹋掉了,你心里又怎样想呢?

恶邮差

亲爱的妈妈,告诉我,为什么你坐在那边地板上,一动也不动,一句话也不说?

雨从打开的窗口洒进来,把你全身都淋湿了,而

① get cross with 〔对…〕生气,发脾气

wet, and you don't mind it.

Do you hear the gong striking four? It is time for my brother to come home from school.

What has happened to you that you look so strange?

Haven't you got a letter from father to-day?

I saw the postman bringing letters in his bag for almost everybody in the town.

Only, father's letters he keeps to read himself. I am sure the postman is a wicked man.

But don't be unhappy about that, mother dear.

To-morrow is market day in the next village. You ask your maid to buy some pens and papers.

I myself will write all father's letters; you will not find a single mistake.

I shall write from A right up to K.

But, mother, why do you smile?

You don't believe that I can write as nicely as father does!

But I shall rule my paper carefully, and write all the letters beautifully big.

When I finish my writing, do you think I shall be so foolish as father and drop it into the **horrid**[①] postman's bag?

I shall bring it to you myself without waiting, and letter by letter help you to read my writing.

I know the postman does not like to give you the really nice letters.

THE END

IT is time for me to go, mother; I am going.

你却毫不在意。

你可听见钟打了四下？该是我哥哥放学回来的时候了。

你的神色这么异乎寻常，究竟发生了什么事啊？

今天你没接到爸爸的来信？

我看见邮差的邮袋里装着许多信，几乎给镇上每个人都送了信去。

只有爸爸写来的信，邮差都留着给他自己看了。我确信这邮差是个恶人。

可是，亲爱的妈妈，你不要因此不开心。

明天是邻村市集的日子。你叫女仆去买笔和纸来。

我亲自来写爸爸的一封家信；管保你找不出一个写错的地方。

我要从 A 字一直写到 K 字。

可是，妈妈，你为什么笑呢？

你不相信我会写得同爸爸一样好？

不过，我会仔细用尺画好线，然后把所有的字母写得又美又大。

① horrid /hɒrɪd/ *a.* 讨厌的,极糟的

我写好了，你以为我会像爸爸那样傻，把信投到那可怕的邮差的邮袋里去吗？

我会立刻亲自给你送去，而且一个字母又一个字母地帮助你读我写的字。

我知道，那邮差是不肯把真正的好信送给你的。

结　局

该是我走的时候了，妈妈；我走了。

When in the **paling**[1] darkness of the lonely dawn you stretch out your arms for your baby in the bed, I shall say, "Baby is not there! "— mother, I am going.

I shall become a delicate draught of air and caress you; and I shall be **ripples**[2] in the water when you bathe, and kiss you and kiss you again.

In the **gusty**[3] night when the rain patters on the leaves you will hear my whisper in your bed, and my laughter will flash with the lightning through the open window into your room.

If you lie awake, thinking of your baby till late into the night, I shall sing to you from the stars, "Sleep mother, sleep."

On the straying moonbeams I shall steal over your bed, and lie upon your **bosom**[4] while you sleep.

I shall become a dream, and through the little opening of your eyelids I shall slip into the depths of your sleep; and when you wake up and look round startled, like a twinkling firefly I shall **flit**[5] out into the darkness.

When, on the great festival of puja, the neighbours' children come and play about the house, I shall melt into the music of the **flute**[6] and **throb**[7] in your heart all day.

Dear auntie will come with puja-presents and will ask, "Where is our baby, sister? Mother, you will tell her softly, "He is in the pupils of my eyes, he is in my body and in my soul."

THE FIRST JASMINES

AH, these **jasmines**[8], these white jasmines!

I seem to remember the first day when I filled my hands with these

① pale /peɪl/ v. 变得苍白;暗淡

② ripple /ˈrɪpl/ n. 涟漪,波痕

③ gusty /ˈɡʌstɪ/ a. 阵风的,刮风的

④ bosom /ˈbʊzəm/ n. 胸部

⑤ flit /flɪt/ v. 迅速飞过

⑥ flute /fluːt/ n. 长笛

⑦ throb /θrɒb/ v.（心脏）跳动,搏动

⑧ jasmine /ˈdʒæsmɪn/ n. 茉莉

你在寂寞黎明的薄暗中伸出手去抱你床上的孩子时，我要告诉你，"孩子不在了！"——妈妈，我走了。

我要变成一缕轻风抚摸你；你沐浴时我要变成水里的涟漪，我要再三地亲你吻你。

大风之夜，雨点潺潺地落在叶子上，这时你会听见我在你床上喁喁细语；而我的笑声，会随着闪电从打开的窗口闪进你的房间。

如果你躺在床上睡不着，想念你的孩子直至深夜，我要从繁星上给你唱歌："睡吧，妈妈，睡吧。"

我要乘明月的游光，偷偷地来到你的床上，在你沉沉入睡时躺在你的胸前。

我要变成一个梦，穿过你眼皮的细缝，溜到你的睡眠深处；当你醒过来，吃惊地向四周张望时，我就像闪烁明灭的萤火虫一样飞到外边儿黑暗中去。

逢到盛大的"难近母祭日"，邻家的孩子都来屋子附近玩耍时，我要融化在笛声里，整天在你心头起伏动荡。

亲爱的姨母带着节日礼物来访，会问你："姐姐，咱们的孩子在哪儿?"妈妈，你会柔声细气地告诉她："他在我的瞳仁里，他在我的身体里和灵魂里。"

第一次手捧素馨花

啊，这些素馨花，这些白色素馨花！

我仿佛还记得我第一天双手捧满这些素馨花，这

jasmines, these white jasmines.

I have loved the sunlight, the sky and the green earth;

I have heard the liquid murmur of the river through the darkness of midnight;

Autumn sunsets have come to me at the bend of a road in the lonely waste, like a bride raising her veil to accept her lover.

Yet my memory is still sweet with the first white jasmines that I held in my hand when I was a child.

Many a glad day has come in my life, and I have laughed with merrymakers on festival nights.

On grey mornings of rain I have **crooned**① many an idle song.

I have worn round my neck the evening wreath of bakulas woven by the hand of love.

Yet my heart is sweet with the memory of the first fresh jasmines that filled my hands when I was a child.

THE BANYAN TREE

O YOU shaggy-headed banyan tree standing on the bank of the pond, have you forgotten the little child, like the birds that have nested in your branches and left you?

Do you not remember how he sat at the window and wondered at the **tangle**② of your roots that plunged underground?

The women would come to fill their jars in the pond, and your huge black shadow would wriggle on the water like sleep struggling to wake up.

Sunlight danced on the ripples like restless tiny shuttles weaving golden **tapestry**③.

些白色素馨花的景象。

我爱阳光，爱天空和苍翠大地。

我听见河流在子夜黑暗里汩汩流动的声音；

秋天的夕阳，在寂寥荒原上大路转弯处迎我，像新娘撩起面纱迎接她的新郎。

然而，我是个孩子时第一次捧在手里的白色素馨花，回忆起来依旧是甜蜜的。

我生平有过许多快乐的日子，节日之夜我曾同逗乐的人一起哈哈大笑。

雨天灰暗的早晨，我曾低吟过许多闲适的诗歌。

我颈子上还戴过爱人亲手用醉花编织的黄昏花环。

然而，回忆起我是个孩子时第一次双手捧满新鲜的素馨花，我的心里依旧是感觉甜蜜的。

榕　树

啊，你挺立在池塘边的蓬头散发的榕树，你可曾忘了那小小的孩子，像小鸟一样在你树枝上筑巢而又离开了你的那个孩子？

你可记得他坐在窗边，对你深入地下的纠结错杂的树根感到诧异？

妇女们常到池边来汲水满罐，你的大黑影便在水面上蠕蠕而动，仿佛睡眠挣扎着要醒过来一样。

阳光在涟漪上闪烁跳动，仿佛不息的小梭子在织着金色的挂毯。

两只鸭子在长着芦苇的池边游动，游在它们自己的影子上，而那孩子静静地坐着遐想。

① croon /kru:n/ v. 低声吟唱

② tangle /'tæŋgl/ n. 纠结的一团,乱糟糟的一堆

③ tapestry /'tæpɪstrɪ/ n. 绣帷,织锦

Two ducks swam by the weedy margin above their shadows, and the child would sit still and think.

He longed to be the wind and blow through your rustling branches, to be your shadow and lengthen with the day on the water, to be a bird and **perch**① on your top-most twig, and to float like those ducks among the weeds and shadows.

THE GIFT

I WANT to give you something, my child, for we are drifting in the stream of the world.

Our lives will be carried apart, and our love forgotten.

But I am not so foolish as to hope that I could buy your heart with my gifts.

Young is your life, your path long, and you drink the love we bring you at one draught and turn and run away from us.

You have your play and your playmates. What harm is there if you have no time or thought for us.

We, indeed, have leisure enough in old age to count the days that are past, to cherish in our hearts what our hands have lost for ever.

The river runs swift with a song, breaking through all barriers. But the mountain stays and remembers, and follows her with his love.

MY SONG

THIS song of mine will **wind**② its music around you, my child, like the fond arms of love.

This song of mine will touch your forehead like a kiss of blessing.

When you are alone it will sit by your side and whisper in your ear,

孩子想成为风，吹过你簌簌的树枝；想成为你的影子，在水面上随着白昼的流光而逐渐伸长；想成为鸟儿，栖息在你的最高枝上；还想同那些鸭子一样，在芦苇与阴影之间浮游。

① perch /pɜːtʃ/ *v.* 栖息

礼　物

我要送点东西给你，我的孩子，因为我们都是漂泊在世界的流水之中的。

我们的生命将被分开，我们的爱将被忘记。

然而我倒没有那么傻，竟指望用礼物来买下你的心。

你的生命正年轻，你的道路是漫长的，你一口气饮下我们带给你的爱，便转过身去，离开我们跑了。

你有你的游戏和你的游伴。如果你无暇同我们在一起，如果你想不到我们，那又何妨！

我们在老年时，确实有足够的闲暇，去计算过去的日子，把手中永远失去的东西，在心里珍爱着。

河流冲破一切堤防，歌唱着迅速流去了。然而山峰留了下来，念念不忘，深情地追忆着。

② wind /waɪnd/ *v.* 绕，缠绕

我的歌

我这歌将以它的音乐萦绕你，我的孩子，犹如深情热爱的双臂。

我这歌将爱抚你的额头，犹如祝福的吻。

你独自一人时，它将坐在你的身旁，在你耳边低语；你在人群之中时，它将像篱笆似的围着你，使你

when you are in the crowd it will fence you about with **aloofness**[1].

My song will be like a pair of wings to your dreams, it will transport your heart to the verge of the unknown.

It will be like the faithful star overhead when dark night is over your road.

My song will sit in the pupils of your eyes, and will carry your sight into the heart of things.

And when my voice is silent in death, my song will speak in your living heart.

① aloofness /əˈluːfnɪs/ *n.*
超然态度

超然绝俗。

我的歌将替你的梦添上翅膀，把你的心载运到未知境界的边缘。

黑夜笼罩你的道路时，它将如忠实的明星在你头上照耀。

我的歌将坐在你眼睛的瞳仁里，使你的目光渗透到万物的内心里。

当我人亡声绝的时候，我的歌将在你生机勃勃的心里说话。

The Gardener

园丁集

1

Servant　HAVE mercy upon your servant, my queen!

Queen　The **assembly**[①] is over and my servants are all gone. Why do you come at this late hour?

Servant　When you have finished with others, that is my time.

I come to ask what remains for your last servant to do.

Queen　What can you expect when it is too late?

Servant　Make me the gardener of your flower garden.

Queen　What folly is this?

Servant　I will give up my other work.

I throw my swords and **lances**[②] down in the dust. Do not send me to distant courts; do not bid me undertake new **conquests**[③]. But make me the gardener of your flower garden.

Queen　What will your duties be?

Servant　The service of your idle days.

I will keep fresh the grassy path where you walk in the morning, where your feet will be greeted with praise at every step by the flowers eager for death.

I will swing you in a swing among the branches of the saptaparna, where the early evening moon will struggle to kiss your skirt through the leaves.

I will **replenish**[④] with **scented**[⑤] oil the lamp that burns by your bedside, and decorate your footstool with sandal and **saffron**[⑥] paste in wondrous designs.

Queen　What will you have for your reward?

一

> **臣仆**　我后，垂怜你的仆人吧！
>
> **皇后**　会议结束了，我的臣子们都散了。你为什么在这样晚的时刻才来呢？
>
> **臣仆**　当你处理完了别人的事，这就挨到我了。
>
> 我来要求的，就是留给你最后一个仆人做的事情。
>
> **皇后**　时候已经太晚了，你还能指望什么呢？
>
> **臣仆**　委派我做你花园里的园丁吧。
>
> **皇后**　这是什么傻劲儿呀？
>
> **臣仆**　我决意放弃我的其他职务。
>
> 我把我的剑与矛委弃在尘土之中。不要派遣我去遥远的宫廷；不要嘱咐我从事新的征伐。但要委派我做你花园里的园丁。
>
> **皇后**　那么你的职责是什么呢？
>
> **臣仆**　侍奉你悠闲的时日。
>
> 我要使你清晨散步的花径永远鲜妍，你的双足，将步步受到甘心舍命的繁花礼赞相迎。
>
> 我要摇荡在七叶树间荡秋千的你，傍晚的月亮将竭力透过树叶来吻你的衣裙。
>
> 我要以香油添满那燃点在你床头的灯；我要以凉鞋、以番红花浆所做的奇妙的图案，装饰你的足凳。
>
> **皇后**　你要求什么作你的酬报呢？
>
> **臣仆**　容我握起你柔嫩如莲花蓓蕾一般的纤手，

① assembly /ə'semblɪ/ *n.* 集会

② lance /lɑːns/ *n.* 长矛

③ conquest /'kɒŋkwest/ *n.* 征服,占领

④ replenish /rɪ'plenɪʃ/ *v.* 把…装满

⑤ scented /'sentɪd/ *a.* 芳香的

⑥ saffron /'sæfrən/ *n.* 藏红花

Servant　To be allowed to hold your little fists like tender lotus-buds and slip flower chains over your wrists; to **tinge**[1] the soles of your feet with the red juice of askoka petals and kiss away the **speck**[2] of dust that may chance to linger there.

Queen　Your prayers are granted, my servant, your will be the gardener of my flower garden.

2

"AH, poet, the evening draws near; your hair is turning grey.

"Do you in your lonely **musing**[3] hear the message of the **hereafter**[4]?"

"It is evening," the poet said, " and I am listening because some one may call from the village, late though it be.

"I watch if young straying hearts meet together, and two pairs of eager eyes beg for music to break their silence and speak for them.

"Who is there to weave their **passionate**[5] songs, if I sit on the shore of life and **contemplate**[6] death and the beyond?

"The early evening star disappears.

"The glow of a funeral **pyre**[7] slowly dies by the silent river.

"Jackals cry in chorus from the courtyard of the deserted house in the light of the worn-out moon.

"If some wanderer, leaving home, come here to watch the night and with bowed head listen to the murmur of the darkness, who is there to whisper the secrets of life into his ears if I shutting my doors, should try to free myself from **mortal**[8] bonds?

"It is a **trifle**[9] that my hair is turning grey.

"I am ever as young or as old as the youngest and the oldest of this

把花环轻轻地套在你的腕上；容我以无忧树花瓣的红汁，染你的脚跖，而且吻掉那偶或滞留在那里的一星尘土。

皇后　我赐你如愿以偿，我的仆人，你将做我花园里的园丁。

二

啊，诗人，黄昏渐近；你的头发在花白了。

在你孤寂的冥想中，你可听到来世的消息？

"是黄昏了，"诗人说，"而我正在谛听，也许村子里有人呼唤，虽然天色已经晚了。

"我留神年轻而失散的心是否已经相聚，两对渴慕的眼睛是否在祈求音乐来打破他们的沉默，替他们诉说衷情。

"如果我坐在人生的海岸上，竟冥想死亡与来世，那么，有谁来编制他们的热情的歌呢？

"早升的黄昏星消失了。

"火葬堆的火光在寂静的河畔慢慢地熄灭了。

"在残月的光华下，豺狼从荒屋的院子里齐声嗥叫。

"如果有什么流浪者，离家来到这儿，通宵无眠，低头听黑暗的喃喃自语；如果我关上大门，竟想摆脱尘世的羁绊，那么，有谁来把人生的秘密悄悄地送进他的耳朵呢？

"我的头发在花白了，那是微不足道的小事。

"我永远跟村子里最年轻的人一样年轻，跟最年迈的人一样年迈。

① tinge /tɪndʒ/ v. 给…染色

② speck /spek/ n. 微粒；一点点

③ musing /'mjuːzɪŋ/ n. 沉思,冥想

④ hereafter /hɪər'ɑːftə(r)/ n. 将来,未来

⑤ passionate /'pæʃənɪt/ a. 热情洋溢的

⑥ contemplate /'kɒntempleɪt/ v. 思量,仔细考虑

⑦ pyre /paɪə/ n.（尤指火葬用的）柴堆

⑧ mortal /'mɔːtəl/ a. 世间的,现世的

⑨ trifle /'traɪfl/ n. 无价值的东西;琐事

village.

"Some have smiles, sweet and simple, and some a sly twinkle in their eyes.

"Some have tears that well up in the daylight, and others tears that are hidden in the **gloom**①.

"They all have need for me, and I have no time to **brood**② over the afterlife.

"I am of an age with each, what matter if my hair turns grey? "

5

I am restless. I am **athirst**③ for **faraway**④ things.

My soul goes out in a longing to touch the skirt of the dim distance.

O Great Beyond, O the keen call of thy **flute**⑤!

I forget, I ever forget, that I have no wings to fly, that I am bound in this spot evermore.

I am eager and wakeful, I am a stranger in a strange land.

Thy breath comes to me whispering an impossible hope.

Thy tongue is known to my heart as its very own.

O Far-to-seek, O the keen call of thy flute!

I forget, I ever forget, that I know not the way, that I have not the winged horse.

I am listless, I am a wanderer in my heart.

In the sunny haze of the **languid**⑥ hours, what vast vision of thine takes shape in the blue of the sky!

O Farthest end, O the keen call of thy flute!

"有的人微笑，甜蜜而且单纯；有的人眼睛里闪烁着狡黠的目光。

"有的人大白天里泪如泉涌；有的人黑夜里掩泣垂泪。

"他们大家都需要我，我无暇思索来世。

"我跟每一个人是同年的，如果我的头发花白了，那又有什么关系呢？"

五

我心绪不宁。我渴望遥远的事物。

我心不在焉，热望着抚摸那昏暗的远方的边缘。

啊，伟大的远方，啊，您那笛子的热烈呼唤呀！

我忘记了，我总是忘记了，我没有飞翔的翅膀，我永远束缚在这一个地方。

我焦灼，我失眠，我是一个异乡的异客。

您吹送给我的气息，悄声微语着一个不可能实现的希望。

我的心领会您的言语，就像领会自己的言语一样。

啊，我所求索的远方，啊，您那笛子的热烈呼唤呀！

我忘记了，我总是忘记了，我不认识路，我没有飞马。

我心绪不宁，我是我自己心里的一个流浪汉。

在慵倦的时刻，烟雾朦胧的阳光下，在天空的一片蔚蓝里，出现了你的何等浩瀚的幻影啊！

啊，遥远的大涯海角，啊，您那笛子的热烈呼唤

① gloom /gluːm/ *n.* 黑暗，昏暗，阴暗

② brood /bruːd/ *v.* 沉思，忧思

③ athirst /əˈθɜːst/ *a.* 渴望的

④ faraway /ˈfɑːrəˈweɪ/ *a.* 遥远的

⑤ flute /fluːt/ *n.* 长笛

⑥ languid /ˈlæŋgwɪd/ *a.* 没精打采的；懒散的

I forget,I ever forget,that the gates are shut everywhere in the house where I dwell alone!

9

When I go alone at night to my love-**tryst**[1], birds do not sing, the wind does not stir, the houses on both sides of the street stand silent.

It is my own **anklets**[2] that grow loud at every step and I am ashamed.

When I sit on my balcony and listen for his footsteps, leaves do not rustle on the trees, and the water is **still**[3] in the river like the sword on the knees of a **sentry**[4] fallen asleep.

It is my own heart that beats wildly—I do not know how to quiet it.

When my love comes and sits by my side, when my body trembles and my eyelids droop, the night darkens, the wind blows out the lamp, and the clouds draw veils over the stars.

It is the jewel at my own breast that shines and gives light. I do not know how to hide it.

11

Come as you are; do not **loiter**[5] over your toilet.

If your braided hair has loosened, if the parting of your hair be not straight, if the ribbons of your **bodice**[6] be not fastened,do not mind.

Come as you are; do not loiter over your toilet.

Come,with quick steps over the grass.

If the **raddle**[7] come from your feet because of the dew,if the rings of bells upon your feet **slacken**[8], if pearls drop out of your chain,do not mind.

呀！

我忘记了，我总是忘记了，在我那独自居住的房子里，门户处处是关着的啊！

九

我在夜间独自去赴爱人约会的时候，鸟儿也不唱了，风也不动了，房子默默地站在街道的两旁。

一步响似一步的是我自己的脚镯，它使我感觉羞涩。

我坐在露台上谛听他足音的时候，树上的叶子寂静无声，河里的流水也凝然不动，正如那睡熟了的哨兵膝上的利剑。

狂野跳动的是我自己的心——我不知道怎样使它平静。

我的爱人来了，坐在我的身旁，我的身体颤抖，我的眼帘下垂的时候，夜黑下来了，风把灯吹灭了，云也给繁星笼上了面纱。

闪烁发光的是我自己胸前的珠宝。我不知道怎样把它遮掩。

一一

你就这样来吧；别把时间消磨在你的梳妆上了。

如果你的辫子松了，如果你的头路分得不直，如果你胸衣上的缎带没有结好，你都不用介意。

你就这样来吧；别把时间消磨在你的梳妆上了。

来吧，以轻盈的脚步越过草地来吧。

如果你脚上的赭石因露水脱色了，如果你脚上的

① tryst /trɪst/ n.（情人的）约会,幽会

② anklet /'æŋklɪt/ n. 脚镯,踝环

③ still /stɪl/ a. 静止的,不动的

④ sentry /'sentrɪ/ n. 哨兵

⑤ loiter /'lɔɪtə/ v. 磨蹭

⑥ bodice /'bɒdɪs/ n. 妇女紧身胸衣

⑦ raddle /'rædl/ n. 红赭石

⑧ slacken /'slækən/ v.（使）松弛;变迟缓

Come with quick steps over the grass.

Do you see the clouds wrapping the sky?

Flocks of **cranes**[1] fly up from the further river-bank and **fitful**[2] gusts of wind rush over the heath.

The anxious cattle run to their **stalls**[3] in the village.

Do you see the clouds wrapping the sky?

In vain you light your toilet lamp—it **flickers**[4] and goes out in the wind.

Who can know that your eyelids have not been touched with lampblack? For your eyes are darker than rain-clouds.

In vain you light your toilet lamp—it goes out.

Come as you are; do not loiter over your toilet.

If the wreath is not woven, who cares; if the wrist-chain has not been linked, let it be.

The sky is overcast with clouds—it is late.

Come as you are; do not loiter over your toilet.

12

If you would be busy and fill your **pitcher**[5], come, O come to my lake.

The water will cling round your feet and **babble**[6] its secret.

The shadow of the coming rain is on the sands, and the clouds hang low upon the blue lines of the trees like the heavy hair above your eyebrows.

I know well the rhythm of your steps, they are beating in my heart.

Come, O come to my lake, if you must fill your pitcher.

铃铛圈儿松了，如果你项链上的珍珠脱落了，你都不用介意。

来吧，以轻盈的脚步越过草地来吧。

你可看见云霾遮蔽着天空？

成群的白鹤从远处河岸向上飞冲，灌木丛生的荒原上奔腾着一阵阵方向不定的狂风。

焦急的牛群向村子里的牛栏直奔。

你可看见云霾遮蔽着天空？

你徒然点亮你梳妆的灯——灯在风中摇曳熄灭了。

谁能知道你的眼皮上没有抹上灯烟呢？因为你的眼睛是比雨云还乌黑啊！

你徒然点亮你梳妆的灯——灯熄灭了。

你就这样来吧；别把时间消磨在你的梳妆上了。

如果花环没有编好，谁在意呢；如果腕上的链子没有接好，那就随它去吧。

天空布满云霾——时间已经不早了。

你就这样来吧；别把时间消磨在你的梳妆上了。

一二

如果你愿意忙碌，愿意盛满你的水罐，来吧，到我的湖边来吧。

湖水将依恋地环抱你的双足，汩汩地诉说它的秘密。

欲来的雨的影子落在沙滩上；云低压在一排排蔚蓝的树木上，正如浓重的头发覆在你的眉毛上。

我十分熟悉你足音的节奏，它动荡在我的心里。

来吧，到我的湖边来吧，如果你一定要盛满你的

① crane /kreɪn/ *n.* 鹤

② fitful /'fɪtful/ *a.* 反复无常的

③ stall /stɔːl/ *n.* 厩，畜栏

④ flicker /'flɪkə/ *v.* 闪烁；摇曳

⑤ pitcher /'pɪtʃə/ *n.* 大水罐

⑥ babble /'bæbl/ *v.* 含糊不清地说

If you would be idle and sit listless and let your pitcher float on the water, come, O come to my lake.

The grassy **slope**① is green, and the wild flowers beyond number.

Your thoughts will stray out of your dark eyes like birds from their nests.

Your **veil**② will drop to your feet.

Come, O come to my lake if you must sit idle.

If you would leave off your play and dive in the water, come, O come to my lake.

Let your blue **mantle**③ lie on the shore; the blue water will cover you and hide you.

The waves will stand a-tiptoe to kiss your neck and whisper in your ears.

Come, O come to my lake, if you would dive in the water.

If you must be mad and leap to your death, come, O come to my lake.

It is cool and **fathomlessly**④ deep.

It is dark like a sleep that is dreamless.

There in its depths nights and days are one, and songs are silence.

Come, O come to my lake, if you would plunge to your death.

14

I was walking by the road, I do not know why, when the noonday was past and bamboo branches rustled in the wind.

The **prone**⑤ shadows with their outstretched arms clung to the feet of the hurrying light.

The koels were **weary**⑥ of their songs.

水罐。

如果你愿意懒散闲坐，并且让你的水罐在水上漂浮，来吧，到我的湖边来吧。

草坡是翠绿的，野花是数不尽的。

你的思想将如鸟儿离巢，从你乌溜溜的眼睛里往外飘浮。

你的面纱将垂落到你的脚边。

来吧，到我的湖边来吧，如果你一定要闲坐。

如果你愿意丢下你的游戏，愿意在水里泅游，来吧，到我的湖边来吧。

把你蓝色的斗篷留在湖岸上吧；蓝蓝的湖水会掩盖你和隐藏你。

波浪将踮起脚来吻你的脖子，在你的耳边悄声细语。

来吧，到我的湖边来吧，如果你愿意在水里泅游。

如果你一定要疯疯癫癫，一定要纵身跳向死亡，来吧，到我的湖边来吧。

湖水冰凉又深不可测。

湖水黑暗如无梦的睡眠。

在那湖水深处，昼夜不分，而歌声就是沉默。

来吧，到我的湖边来吧，如果你愿意投水自沉。

一四

中午已逝，竹枝在风中萧萧摇曳，我在路旁踯躅，不知道为了什么。

俯伏的树影伸出手臂，挽住匆匆日光的双足。

布谷唱厌了它们的歌曲。

① slope /sləʊp/ *n.* 山坡

② veil /veɪl/ *n.* 面纱

③ mantle /'mæntl/ *n.* 披风,斗篷

④ fathomless /'fæðəmlɪs/ *a.* 深不可测的;不可了解的

⑤ prone /prəʊn/ *a.* 向前俯的,倾斜的

⑥ weary /'wɪərɪ/ *a.* 疲倦的;困乏的

I was walking by the road, I do not know why.

The **hut**[①] by the side of the water is shaded by an overhanging tree.

Some one was busy with her work, and her **bangles**[②] made music in the corner.

I stood before this hut, I know not why.

The narrow **winding**[③] road crosses many a mustard field, and many a mango forest.

It passes by the temple of the village and the market at the river landing place.

I stopped by this hut, I do not know why.

Years ago it was a day of breezy March when the murmur if the spring was **languorous**[④], and mango blossoms were dropping on the dust.

The rippling water leapt and licked the brass vessel that stood on the landing step.

I think of that day of breezy March, I do not know why.

Shadows are deepening and cattle returning to their folds.

The light is grey upon the lonely **meadows**[⑤], and the village are waiting for the ferry at the bank.

I slowly return upon my steps, I do not know why.

15

I run as a musk-deer runs in the shadow of the forest mad with his own perfume.

The night is the night of mid-May, the breeze is the breeze of the south.

I lose my way and I wander, I seek what I cannot get, I get what I

我在路旁踯躅，不知道为了什么。

亭亭如盖的树，遮阴着那水边的茅屋。

有一个人在忙着她的工作，她的手镯在角落里发出音乐。

我兀立在那茅屋的门前，不知道为了什么。

曲折的小径，通过好些芥菜田，好些芒果林。

它经过了村里的庙宇，码头边的市集。

我停留在那茅屋的门前，不知道为了什么。

那是多年前微风和煦的三月天，那时候春的细语是慵倦的，芒果花正掉落在尘土上。

粼粼的水波激荡，水花舐吻着放在河埠踏级上的铜壶。

我想起了微风和煦的三月天，不知道为了什么。

夜影渐浓，牛羊也回栏了。

孤寂的草原上暮色苍茫，村里人在河边等着渡船。

我缓步回去，不知道为了什么。

一五

我飞跑如一头麝香鹿：因为自己的香气而发狂，飞跑在森林的阴影里。

夜是五月中旬的夜，风是南来的风。

我迷失了我的路，我彷徨歧途，我求索我得不到的，我得到了我不求索的。

我自己的欲望的形象，从我的心里走出来，手舞足蹈。

闪烁的幻象倏忽地飞翔。

① hut /hʌt/ n. （简陋的）小屋

② bangle /'bæŋgl/ n. 手镯，脚镯

③ winding /'waɪndɪŋ/ a. 曲折的

④ languorous /'læŋgərəs/ a. 怠惰的，没精打采的

⑤ meadow /'medəʊ/ n. 草地，牧场

do not seek.

From my heart comes out and dances the image of my own desire.

The gleaming vision flits on.

I try to clasp it firmly, it eludes me and leads me astray.

I seek what I cannot get, I get what I do not seek.

16

Hands cling to hands and eyes linger on eyes; thus begins the record of our hearts.

It is the moonlit night of March; the sweet smell of **henna**[1] is in the air; my flute lies on the earth **neglected**[2] and your garland of flowers is unfinished.

This love between you and me is simple as a song.

Your veil of the **saffron**[3] colour makes my eyes drunk.

The jasmine wreath that you wove me thrills to my heart like praise.

It is a game of giving and withholding, **revealing**[4] and screening again; some smiles and some little shyness, and some sweet useless struggles.

This love between you and me is simple as a song.

No mystery beyond the present; no striving for the impossible; no shadow behind the charm; no **groping**[5] in the depth of the dark.

This love between you and me is simple as a song.

We do not stray out of all words into the ever silent; we do not raise our hands to the **void**[6] for things beyond hope.

It is enough what we give and we get.

We have not crushed the joy to the utmost to **wring**[7] from it the

我要把它牢牢抓住，它躲开了我，它把我引入了歧途。

我求索我得不到的，我得到了我不求索的。

一六

两手相挽，凝眸相视：这样开始了我们的心的记录。

这是三月的月明之夜；空气里是指甲花的甜香；我的横笛遗忘在大地上，而你的花环也没有编成。

你我之间的这种爱，单纯如歌曲。

你的番红花色的面纱，使我醉眼陶然。

你为我编的素馨花冠，像赞美似的使我心迷神驰。

这是一种欲予故夺、欲露故藏的游戏；一些微笑，一些微微的羞怯，还有一些甜蜜的无用的挣扎。

你我之间的这种爱，单纯如歌曲。

没有超越现实的神秘；没有对不可能事物的强求；没有藏在魅力背后的阴影；也没有在黑暗深处的摸索。

你我之间的这种爱，单纯如歌曲。

我们并不背离一切言语而走入永远缄默的歧途；我们并不向虚空伸手要求超乎冀望的事物。

我们所给予的和我们所得到的，都已经足够。

我们不曾过度地从欢乐中压榨出痛苦的醇酒。

你我之间的这种爱，单纯如歌曲。

① henna /'henə/ n. 指甲花

② neglect /nɪ'glekt/ v. 遗漏

③ saffron /'sæfrən/ a. 藏红花色的

④ reveal /rɪ'viːl/ v. 显示；露出；泄露；透露

⑤ grope /grəup/ v. 摸索；探索

⑥ void /vɔɪd/ n. 空白，空虚

⑦ wring /rɪŋ/ v. 尽力索取，强行取得

wine of pain.

This love between you and me is simple as a song.

17

The yellow birds sing in their tree and makes my heart dance with gladness.

We both live in the same village, and that is our one piece of joy.

Her pair of pet lambs come to **graze**[①] in the shade of our garden trees.

If they stray into my barley field, I take them up in my arms.

The name of our village is Khanjana, and Anjana they call our river.

My name is known to all the village, and her name is Ranjana.

Only one field lies between us.

Bees that have **hived**[②] in our grove go to seek honey in theirs.

Flowers **launched**[③] from their landing-stairs come floating by the stream where we bathe.

Baskets of dried kusm flowers come from their fields to our market.

The name of our village is Khanjana, and Anjana they call our river.

My name is known to all the village, and her name is Ranjana.

The lane that winds to their house is fragrant in the spring with mango flowers.

When their **linseed**[④] is ripe for harvest the **hemp**[⑤] is in bloom in our field.

The stars that smile on their cottage send us the same twinkling look.

The rain that floods their tank makes glad our kadam forest.

一七

黄鸟在她们的树上歌唱，使我的心欢腾雀跃。

我们俩同住在一个村子里，那就是我们的一桩欢喜。

她宠爱的一对羊羔，来到我们花园里树荫下吃草。

如果羊羔闯进了我们的大麦田，我就双手把羊羔抱起。

我们村子的名字叫卡荫那，大家管我们的河流叫安荫那。

我的名字全村都知道，她的名字叫兰荫娜。

我们之间只隔着一块田地。

在我们的小树林里作窠的蜜蜂，到她们的小树林里采蜜。

从她们的河埠上扔下去的花朵，浮到我们洗澡的溪流里。

一篮篮干燥的红花，从她们的田野里来到我们的市集上。

我们村子的名字叫卡荫那，大家管我们的河流叫安荫那。

我的名字全村都知道，她的名字叫兰荫娜。

曲曲折折通到她家门口的小巷，春天里充满了芒果花的芳香。

她们的亚麻子成熟到可以收割的时候，大麻在我们的田里开花。

在她们的茅屋上微笑的繁星，送给我们同样荧荧发亮的眼光。

涨满了她们池塘的春雨，也使我们的迦昙波树林

① graze /greɪz/ v.（牛、羊等）吃青草

② hive /haɪv/ v.（蜂）进入蜂箱

③ launch /lɔːntʃ/ v. 发出

④ linseed /ˈlɪnsiːd/ n. 亚麻籽

⑤ hemp /hemp/ n. 棕榈

The name of our village is Khanjana, and Anjana they call our river.

My name is known to all the village, and her name is Ranjana.

19

You walked by the riverside path with the full pitcher upon your hip.

Why did you swiftly turn your face and **peep**[1] at me through your **fluttering**[2] veil?

That **gleaming**[3] look from the dark came upon me like a breeze that sends a shiver through the sipping water and sweeps away to the shadowy shore.

It came to me like a bird of the evening that hurriedly flies across the lampless room from the one open window to the other, and disappears in the night.

You are hidden like a star behind the hills, and I am a passer-by upon the road.

But why did you stop for a moment and glance at my face through your veil while you walked by the riverside path with the full pitcher upon your hip?

21

Why did he choose to come to my door, the wandering youth, when the day **dawned**[4]?

As I come in and out I pass by him every time, and my eyes are caught by his face.

I know not if I should speak to him or keep silent. Why did he choose to come to my door.

欢欣。

我们村子的名字叫卡旃那，大家管我们的河流叫安旃那。

我的名字全村都知道，她的名字叫兰旃娜。

一九

满满的水罐靠着臀部，你在河滨小径上走过。

你为什么迅速地转过脸来，透过飘扬的面纱偷偷地投我一瞥呢？

你从黑暗中投到我身上的明亮眼光，像一丝微风，送一阵战栗透过粼粼的水波，又吹向朦胧的岸边。

你投到我身上的眼光，像黄昏时分的飞鸟，匆忙地穿越没有灯火的房间，从一个开着的窗子进去，从另一个开着的窗子出来，便消失在黑夜里了。

你隐藏如群山后面的一颗星星，而我是大路上的一个过客。

可是，满满的水罐靠着臀部，你在河滨小径上走过的时候，你为什么要驻足片刻，透过面纱瞅我的脸呢？

二一

天色方曙的时候，这个彷徨的年轻人，为什么他偏要来到我的门口呢？

我每次走出走进都从他身边经过，而他的脸又吸住了我的眼睛。

我不知道我应该跟他说话还是保持沉默。为什么他偏要来到我的门口呢？

七月里多云的夜是黝黑的；秋季里的天空是蓝得柔和的；南风骀荡的春日是心神不定的。

① peep /piːp/ *v.* 偷偷一瞥
② fluttering /flʌtərɪŋ/ *a.* 飘扬的,飘动的

③ gleaming /gliːmɪŋ/ *a.* 明亮的

④ dawn /dɔːn/ *v.* 破晓

The cloudy nights in July are dark; the sky is soft blue in the autumn; the spring days are restless with the south wind.

He weaves his songs with fresh tunes every time.

I turn from my work and my eyes fill with the mist. Why did he choose to come my door?

22

When she passed by me with quick steps, the end of her skirt touched me.

From the unknown island of a heart came a sudden warm breath of spring.

A flutter of a flitting touch brushed me and vanished in a moment, like a torn flower petal blown in the breeze.

It fell upon my heart like a sigh of her body and whisper of her heart.

26

"What comes from? your willing hands I take. I beg for nothing more."

"Yes, yes, I know you, modest mendicant, you ask for all that one has."

"If there be a **stray**[①] flower for me I will wear it in my heart."

"But if there be thorns? "

"I will **endure**[②] them."

"Yes, yes, I know you, modest **mendicant**[③], you ask for all that one has."

"If but once you should raise your loving eyes to my face it would

每次他都用新鲜的曲调编制他的歌曲。

我搁下我的工作，而我的眼睛矇矇眬眬。为什么他偏要来到我的门口呢？

二二

她快步从我身边经过的时候，她的衣裙的边缘触到了我。

从一颗心的未知的岛上，吹来了一丝突如其来的、温暖的、春天的气息。

衣裙的飘忽的接触，轻拂即逝，仿佛那撕掉的花瓣飘扬在微风里。

这飘忽的接触落在我的心上，仿佛就是她肉体的叹息和心灵的低诉。

二六

"我收受你自愿的手所给予的。我别无他求。"

"是的，是的，谦和的求乞者，我懂得你，你要求的是人家所有的一切。"

"如果有一朵飘零的落花给我，我就戴在我的心上。"

"但如果花上有刺呢？"

"我就忍受。"

"是的，是的，谦和的求乞者，我懂得你，你要求的是人家所有的一切。"

"如果你抬起爱恋的眼睛瞧我的脸，哪怕只是一次，也会使我终身甜蜜，死后犹甜。"

"但如果只是残酷的眼色呢？"

"我就留着它刺透我的心。"

"是的，是的，谦和的求乞者，我懂得你，你要求的是人家所有的一切。"

① stray /streɪ/ *a.* 独自的;走失的

② endure /ɪn'djuə/ *v.* 忍受,忍耐

③ mendicant /'mendikənt/ *n.* 乞丐

make my life sweet beyond death."

"But if there be only cruel glances? "

"I will keep them **piercing**① my heart."

"Yes, yes, I know you, modest mendicant, you ask for all that one has."

27

"Trust love even if it brings sorrow. Do not close up your heart."

"Ah no, my friend, your words are dark, I cannot understand them."

"The heart is only giving away with a tear and a song, my love."

"Ah no, my friend, your words are dark, I cannot understand them."

"Pleasure is **frail**② like a dewdrop, while it laughs it dies. But sorrow is strong and **abiding**③. Let sorrowful love wake in your eyes."

"Ah no, my friend, your words are dark, I cannot understand them."

"The **lotus**④ blooms in the sight of the sun, and loses all that it has. It would not remain in **bud**⑤ in the **eternal**⑥ winter mist."

"Ah no, my friend, your words are dark, I cannot understand them."

28

Your questioning eyes are sad. They seem to know my meaning as the moon would **fathom**⑦ the sea.

I have bared my life before your eyes from end to end, with nothing hidden or held back. That is why you know me not.

If it were only a gem I could break it into a hundred pieces and string them into a chain to put on your neck.

If it were only a flower, round and small and sweet, I could pluck it from its stem to set it in your hair.

二七

"相信爱，即使它给你带来悲哀也要相信爱。别深锁紧闭你的心。"

"啊，不，我的朋友，你的话是玄妙的，我不能够了解它们的意义。"

"心就是为了交给别人的，伴随着一滴眼泪和一支歌曲，我的爱人。"

"啊，不，我的朋友，你的话是玄妙的，我不能够了解它们的意义。"

"快乐像露水一样脆弱，大笑之际就消失无遗。但悲哀是坚强而持久的。让悲哀的爱在你的眼睛里醒来。"

"啊，不，我的朋友，你的话是玄妙的，我不能够了解它们的意义。"

"莲花在太阳的眼光下开放，因而失掉了它所有的一切。于是它就不会在永远的冬日之雾里始终含苞待放。"

"啊，不，我的朋友，你的话是玄妙的，我不能够了解它们的意义。"

二八

你询问的眼睛是悲伤的。你的眼睛要探索我心里的意思，正如月亮要探测大海的深浅。

我已经把我的生活自始至终暴露在你的眼前，毫无隐藏，也毫无保留。这就是你为什么不了解我的缘故。

如果它只是一块宝石，我就能把它打成碎片，串成项链，戴在你的脖子上。

如果它只是一朵花，圆圆的，玲珑而又芳香，我就能把它从花茎上摘下来，缀在你的头发上。

① pierce /pɪəs/ v. 刺入；刺穿，穿透

② frail /freɪl/ a. 脆弱的

③ abiding /ə'baɪdɪŋ/ a. 持久的，永久的

④ lotus /'ləʊtəs/ n. 莲，莲花

⑤ bud /bʌd/ n. 苞，花蕾

⑥ eternal /ɪ't3ːnəl/ a. 永恒的，永久的

⑦ fathom /'fæðəm/ v. 测量

But it is a heart, my beloved. Where are its shores and its bottom?

You know not the limits of this kingdom, still you are its queen.

If it were only a moment of pleasure it would flower in an easy smile, and you could see it and read it in a moment.

If it were merely a pain it would melt in **limpid**[①] tears, reflecting its inmost secret without a word.

But it is love, my beloved.

Its pleasure and pain are boundless, and endless its wants and wealth.

It is as near to you as your life, but you can never wholly know it.

30

You are the evening cloud floating in the sky of my dreams.

I paint you and **fashion**[②] you ever with my love longings.

You are my own, my own, Dweller in my endless dreams!

Your feet are rosy-red with the glow of my heart's desire, Gleaner of my sunset songs!

Your lips are bitter-sweet with the taste of my wine of pain.

You are my own, my own, Dweller in my lonesome dreams!

With the shadow of my passion have I darken your eyes, Haunter of the depth of my gaze!

I have caught you and wrapt you, my love, in the net of my music.

You are my own, my own, Dweller in my deathless dreams!

31

My heart, the bird of the wilderness, has found its sky in your eyes.

They are the cradle of the morning, they are the kingdom of the stars.

然而它是一颗心啊，我的亲爱的。哪儿是它的边哪儿是它的底呢？

你不知道这王国的疆界，而你仍然是这王国的皇后。

如果它只是片刻的欢乐，它就会在悠然的一笑中绽成花朵，而你就能在刹那间看到它领会它。

如果它只是一种痛苦，它就会溶化成晶莹的泪珠，不用说一句话就反映出最隐秘的秘密。

然而它是爱啊，我的亲爱的。

它的欢乐和痛苦是无限的，而无穷的是它的贫乏和富足。

它像你的生命一样的贴近你，然而你永远不能完全了解它啊。

三〇

你是在我的梦的天空里飘浮着的晚霞。

我永远用爱的渴望来描绘和塑造你的形象。

我无穷的梦里的居民啊，你是我的亲亲，我的亲亲！

我的夕阳之歌的采集人啊，你的双足因我心头欲望的霞光而嫣红。

你的嘴唇因我痛苦的酒味而甜苦。

我孤寂的梦的居民啊，你是我的亲亲，我的亲亲！

出没在我凝眸睇视里的人儿啊，我已经用我热情的阴影，染黑了你的眼睛。

我的爱人啊，我已经用我音乐的网，逮住了你，裹住了你。

我不朽的梦里的居民啊，你是我的亲亲，我的亲亲。

三一

我的心是旷野的鸟，已经在你的眼睛里找到了天空。

① limpid /ˈlɪmpɪd/ a. 清澈的,透明的

② fashion /ˈfæʃən/ v. 把…塑造成

My songs are lost in their depths.

Let me but soar in that sky, in its lonely immensity.

Let me but **cleave**① its clouds and spread wings in its sunshine.

32

Tell me if this be all true, my lover, tell me if this be true.

When these eyes flash their lightning the dark clouds in your breast make stormy answer.

Is it true that my lips are sweet like the opening bud of the first conscious love?

Do the memories of vanished months of May linger in my limbs?

Does the earth, like a harp, **shiver**② into songs with the touch of my feet?

Is it then true that the dewdrops fall from the eyes of night when I am seen, and the morning light is glad when it wraps my body round?

Is it true, is it true, that your love travelled alone through ages and worlds in search of me?

That when you found me at last, your age-long desire found utter peace in my gentle speech and my eyes and lips and flowing hair?

Is it then true that the mystery of the Infinite is written on this little forehead of mine?

Tell me, my lover, if all this be true.

35

Lest I should know you too easily, you play with me.

You blind me with flashes of laughter to hide your tears.

I know, I know your art.

You never say the word you would.

你的眼睛是早晨的摇篮，你的眼睛是繁星的王国。

我的歌曲，消失在你眼睛的深处。

就让我翱翔在那一片天空里，翱翔在那一片孤寂无垠的空间里。

就让我排开它那朵朵的云彩，在它的阳光里展翅飞翔。

三二

告诉我，这一切可是真的，我的爱人，这可是真的？

当我的眼睛闪射出电光，你胸中的乌云就报之以风暴？

我的嘴唇，真的像那第一次意识到的爱在蓓蕾方绽时一样的甜蜜？

那逝去的五月的记忆，竟还萦绕在我的手足之间？

我的双脚接触大地时，大地竟为之震动，像竖琴一样响起了音乐？

那么，黑夜看见了我便眼睛里掉下露水，晨曦拥抱了我的身体便欢欣喜悦，可又是真的吗？

这可是真的，这可是真的，你的爱竟历尽千年万代、走遍天涯海角，独自来找寻我吗？

当你终于找到了我的时候，你那年深月久的热情，真的也就在我的温柔的言语、眼睛、嘴唇和飘垂的头发里，找到了完满的安宁吗？

那么，"无限"的神秘就写在我渺小的额角上，可又是真的吗？

告诉我，我的爱人，这一切可是真的？

三五

生怕我不费功夫就懂得你：你就故意逗弄我。

你用笑声的闪光使我的眼睛迷眩，从而掩饰你的

① cleave /kli:v/ v. 劈开，剁开

② shiver /'ʃɪvə/ v. 颤抖，哆嗦

Lest I should not prize you, you **elude**① me in a thousand ways.

Lest I should confuse you with the crowd, you stand aside.

I know, I know your art.

You never walk the path you would.

Your claim is more than that of others, that is why you are silent.

With playful carelessness you avoid my gifts.

I know, I know your art.

You never will take what you would.

37

Would you put your wreath of fresh flowers on my neck, fair one?

But you must know that the one **wreath**② that I had woven is for the many, for those who are seen in glimpses, or dwell in lands unexplored, or live in poets' songs.

It is too late to ask my heart in return for yours.

There was a time when my life was like a bud, all its perfume was stored in its core.

Now it is **squandered**③ far and wide.

Who knows the **enchantment**④ that can gather and shut it up again?

My heart is not mine to give to one only, it is given to the many.

38

My love, once upon a time your poet launched a great epic in his mind.

Alas, I was not careful, and it struck your ringing anklets and came to grief.

It broke up into scraps of songs and lay scattered at your feet.

① elude /ɪ'lju:d/ v. 逃避，
躲避

眼泪。

我知道，我知道你的巧计，

你从来不说你心里要说的话。

生怕我不珍爱你：你就千方百计地躲避我。

生怕我把你与众人混淆不清，你就站在一边。

我知道，我知道你的巧计，

你从来不走你心里要走的路。

你的要求超过了别人的，那就是你为什么缄默的缘故。

你用玩笑的漫不经心的神情回避了我的礼物。

我知道，我知道你的巧计，

你从来不接受你心里要接受的东西。

② wreath /ri:θ/ n. 花环，花圈

三七

"美人，把你的鲜花环挂在我的脖子上，好吗?"

可是你必须知道，我已经编好的那一个花环，是为了许多人编的，为那些只在一瞥间见到的人，或者是住在没有开发过的地方的人，生活在诗人的诗歌里的人。

要求我的心酬答你的心，是已经太晚了。

③ squander /'skwɔndə/ v. 浪费，乱花

④ enchantment /ɪn'tʃæntmənt/ n. 魅力，迷人之处

有过一个时候，我的生命像蓓蕾，一切芳香都贮藏在核心里。

现在可已经散之四方了。

谁知道那个能够把它重新收集和封藏起来的魔法呢?

我的心不是我自己的、仅仅献给一个人的心，我的心是献给许多人的。

三八

我的爱人，从前你的诗人的心灵里，有一首伟大

All my cargo of the stories of old wars was tossed by the laughing waves and **soaked**[①] in tears and sank.

You must make this loss good to me, my love.

If my claims to **immortal**[②] fame after death are **shattered**[③], make me immortal while I live.

And I will not **mourn**[④] for my loss nor blame you.

39

I try to weave a wreath all the morning, but the flowers slip and they drop out.

You sit there watching me in secret through the corner of your prying eyes.

Ask those eyes, darkly planning mischief, whose fault it was.

I try to sing a song, but in vain.

A hidden smile trembles on your lips, ask of it the reason of my failure.

Let your smiling lips say on oath how my voice lost itself in silence like a drunken bee in the lotus.

It is evening, and the time for the flowers to chose their petals.

Give me how to sit by your side, and bid my lips to do the work that can be done in silence and in dim light of stars.

40

An unbelieving smile flits on your eyes when I come to you to take my leave.

I have done it so often that you think I will soon return.

To tell you the truth I have the same doubt in my mind.

的史诗在航行。

咳，我一个不留神，它就触着了你叮当的脚镯，落了个悲哀的结局。

它碎成零落残破的歌，零乱地散落在你的脚下。

我所载运的一切古代战争的故事，被哗笑的波浪摇撼震荡，浸透了泪水，沉没了。

你一定得赔偿我这个损失，我的爱人。

如果我对死后名垂不朽的期望是破灭了，你就使我在活着的时候不朽吧。

那么，我就决不惋惜我的损失，我就决不责备你。

三九

我整个儿早晨要想编一个花环，可是花朵腻滑难缀，纷纷掉落了。

你坐在那儿，你窥探的眼睛偷偷瞟着我。

问问这双暗暗策划着恶作剧的眼睛吧，这究竟是谁的过失？

我要想唱一个歌，可是唱不成。

一个隐约的微笑悸动在你的嘴唇上；你向它追问我失败的原因吧。

让你微笑的嘴唇对天起誓：我的歌声是怎样的消失在沉默里，正如醉醺醺的蜜蜂消失在莲花里。

是黄昏了，是花朵合上花瓣的时候了。

允许我坐在你的身边，嘱咐我的嘴唇做那在静默中在朦胧的星光里所能做的事吧。

四〇

当我来告别的时候，一丝怀疑的微笑掠过你的眼睛。

我来告别的次数太多了，所以你认为我不久就会

① soak /səuk/ v. 浸,泡
② immortal /ɪˈmɔːtl/ a. 永世的,不朽的
③ shatter /ˈʃætə/ v. 破裂
④ mourn /mɔːn/ v. 哀悼

For the spring days come again time after time; the full moon takes leave and comes on another visit, the flower come again and blush upon their branches year after year, and it is likely that I take my leave only to come to you again.

But keep the **illusion**① awhile; do not send it away with ungentle haste.

When I say I leave you for all time, accept it as true, and let a mist of tears for one moment deepen the dark rim of your eyes.

Then smile as **archly**② as you like when I come again.

44

Reverend③ sir, forgive this pair of **sinners**④.

Spring winds to-day are blowing in wild eddies, driving dust and dead leaves away, and with them your lessons are all lost.

Do not say, father, that life is a **vanity**⑤.

For me have made truce with death for once, and only for a few fragrant hours we two have been made immortal.

Even if the king's army came and fiercely fell upon us we should sadly shake our heads and say, Brothers, you are disturbing us. If you must have this noisy game, go and clatter your arms elsewhere.

Since only for a few **fleeting**⑥ moments we have been made immortal.

If friendly people came and flocked around us, we should humbly bow to them and say, This **extravagant**⑦ good fortune is an embarrassment to us. Room is scare in the infinite sky where we dwell. For in the springtime flowers come in crowds, and the busy wings of bees **jostle**⑧ each other. Our little heaven, where dwell only we two

回来的哩。

跟你说老实话吧，我自己心里也有同样的怀疑。

因为春日去而复来；圆月别后重访，而年复一年，繁花重发，嫣红枝头；我的辞行呢，仿佛也只是为了重新来到你的身边。

暂时保留着这幻想吧，不要粗率地把它匆匆送走。

当我说我要永远离开你了，你就把它当作真话，让泪水的雾暂时加深你黑色的眼眶吧。

你再尽情地娇笑吧，当我重来的时候。

四四

长老，饶恕这一对罪人吧。

今天春风在狂野地疾卷奔腾，卷走了尘土，卷走了枯叶；于是你的教训也随着尘土和枯叶而消失了。

长老，不要说人生是空虚的。

因为我们已经一度与死亡互不相犯，我们俩仅仅在这几个芬芳的时辰里就得到了永生。

哪怕开来了国王的军队，猛烈地攻击我们，我们也要悲哀地摇摇头，说："兄弟们，你们在打搅我们了。如果你们一定要玩这喧闹的游戏，到别处去动你们的干戈吧。

因为我们只是在稍纵即逝的片刻里得到了永生。"

如果友好的人们围拢来了，我们也要谦恭地向他们鞠躬，说："这放浪形骸的好运对于我们是件窘迫的事。我们所居住的无穷的天空里，缺少转身的余地。因为春天里繁花成群地开放，蜜蜂忙碌的翅膀彼此冲撞。我们的小小的天堂，只住着我们这两个不朽的人

① illusion /ɪ'ljuːʒən/ n. 错觉,幻想

② archly /'ɑːtʃlɪ/ adv. 顽皮地;淘气地

③ reverend /'revərənd/ a. 可尊敬的(对牧师或神父的尊称)

④ sinner /'sɪnə/ n. 罪人

⑤ vanity /'vænɪtɪ/ n. 虚荣心;空虚,无价值

⑥ fleeting /'fliːtɪŋ/ a. 疾驰的,飞逝的

⑦ extravagant /ɪk'strævəgənt/ a. 奢侈的,挥霍的

⑧ jostle /'dʒɒsəl/ v. 挤,推,撞

immortals, is too **absurdly**[①] narrow.

49

I hold her hands and press her to my breast.

I try to fill my arms with her loveliness, to plunder her sweet smile with kisses, to drink her dark glances with my eyes.

Ah, but, where is it? Who can strain the blue from the sky?

I try to grasp the beauty, it **eludes**[②] me, leaving only the body in my hands.

Baffled and weary I come back.

How can the body touch the flower which only the spirit may touch?

57

I **plucked**[③] your flower, O world!

I pressed it to my heart and the thorn pricked.

When the day waned and it darkened, I found that the flower had faded, but the pain remained.

More flowers will come to you with perfume and pride, O world!

But my time for flower-gathering is over, and through the dark night I have not my rose, only the pain remains.

59

O woman, you are not merely the handiwork of God, but also of men; these are ever endowing you with beauty from their hearts.

Poets are weaving for you a web with threads of golden imagery; painters are giving your form ever new immortality.

① absurdly /əb'sɜ:dlɪ/ *ad.*
荒谬地,荒唐地

② clude /ɪ'lu:d/ *v.* 避开,逃
避,躲避

③ pluck /plʌk/ *v.* 采,摘;
拔

的地方，是狭窄得太可笑了啊。"

四九

我握住她的手，把她紧抱在我的怀里。

我想以她的美丽充实我的怀抱，以接吻劫掠她的甜笑，以我的眼睛畅饮她的黑黝黝的眼色。

啊，可是，它在哪儿呢？谁能强取天空的蔚蓝呢？

我竭力要把捉住美；美躲开了我，只留下肉体在我的手里。

我回来了，挫败了也疲倦了。

肉体怎么能接触那只有精神可以接触的花朵呢？

五七

宇宙啊，我采撷你的花朵。

我把花紧抱在心头，而花的刺却刺痛了我。

当白昼消逝、天色暗下来的时候，我发觉花已经萎谢了，但痛苦依然存在。

宇宙啊，更多的花朵将带着芳香和妍丽来到你的身边。

但我采集花朵的时机是过去了；没有玫瑰，只有滞留的痛苦伴我度过长夜。

五九

女人啊，你不仅是神的杰作，而且也是男人的杰作；这些人永远在从他们心里把美丽赋予你。

诗人在以金色的幻想的线为你织网；画家在给你的形体以永久常新的不朽。

The sea gives its pearls, the mines their gold, the summer gardens their flowers to **deck**[①] you, to cover you, to make you more precious.

The desire of men's hearts has shed its glory over your youth.

You are one half woman and one half dream.

61

Peace, my heart, let the time for the parting be sweet.

Let it not be a death but completeness.

Let love melt into memory and pain into songs.

Let the flight through the sky end in the folding of the wings over the nest.

Let the last touch of your hands be gentle like the flower of the night.

Stand still, O Beautiful End, for a moment, and say your last words in silence.

I bow you and hold up my lamp to light you on your way.

63

Traveller, must you go?

The night is still and the darkness **swoons**[②] upon the forest.

The lamps are bright in our balcony, the flowers all fresh, and the youthful eyes still awake.

Is the time for your parting come?

Traveller, must you go?

We have not bound your feet with our entreating arms.

Your doors are open. Your horse stands saddled at the gate.

If we have tried to bar your passage it was but with our songs.

大海献出珍珠，矿山献出金子，夏天的花园献出花朵，来装饰你、遮掩你，使你更加珍贵。

男子心里的欲望，把它的光辉洒遍了你的青春。

你一半是女人一半是梦。

六一

安静吧，我的心，让这分别的时刻成为甜蜜的。

让它不成为死而成为完满。

让爱融成回忆，而痛苦化成歌曲。

让冲天的翱翔终之以归巢敛翅。

让你的手的最后的接触，温柔如夜间的花朵。

美丽的终局啊，站住一忽儿，在缄默中说出你最后的话吧。

我向你鞠躬，而且举起我的灯给你照亮道路。

六三

旅人，你一定要走吗？

夜是静谧的，黑暗昏睡在树林上。

露台上灯火辉煌，繁花朵朵鲜丽，年轻的眼睛也还是清醒的。

是你离别的时候到了吗？

旅人，你一定要走吗？

我们不曾以恳求的手臂束缚你的双足。

你的门是开着的。你的马上了鞍子站在门口。

如果我们曾设法挡住你的去路，那也不过是用我们的歌曲罢了。

如果我们曾设法阻拦你，那也不过是用我们的眼

① deck /dek/ v. 装饰，打扮

② swoon /swuːn/ v. 〈文〉昏厥，昏倒

Did we ever try to hold you back it was but with our eyes.

Traveller, we are helpless to keep you. We have only our tears.

What quenchless fire glows in your eyes?

What restless fever runs in your blood?

What call from the dark urges you?

What awful **incantation**① have you read among the stars in the sky, that with a sealed secret message the night entered your heart, silent and strange?

If you do not care for merry meetings, if you must have peace, weary heart, we shall put our lamps out and silence our harps.

We shall sit still in the dark in the **rustle**② of leaves, and the tired moon will shed pale rays on your window.

O traveller, what sleepless spirit has touched you from the heart of the midnight?

64

I spent my day on the **scorching**③ hot dust of the road.

Now, in the cool of the evening, I knock at the door of the inn. It is deserted and in ruins.

A grim ashath tree spreads its hungry **clutching**④ roots through the gaping **fissures**⑤ of the walks.

Days have been when wayfarers came here to wash their weary feet.

They spread their mats in the courtyard in the dim light of the early moon, and sat and talked of strange lands.

They woke refreshed in the morning when birds made them glad, and friendly flowers nodded their heads at them from the wayside.

But no lighted lamp awaited me when I came here.

睛罢了。

旅人，要留住你我们是无能为力的。我们只有眼泪。

是什么不灭的火在你眼睛里灼灼发亮？

是什么不安的狂热在你的血液里奔腾？

黑暗中有什么呼唤在催促你？

你在天空的繁星间读到了什么可怕的咒语，黑夜乃带着封缄的密讯，进入了你沉默而古怪的心？

疲倦的心啊，如果你不爱欢乐的聚会，如果你一定要安静，我们就灭掉我们的灯，也不再弹奏我们的竖琴。

我们就静静地坐在黑暗中的叶声萧萧里，而疲倦的月亮就会把苍白的光华洒在你的窗子上。

旅人啊，是什么不眠的精灵从子夜的心里触动了你呢？

六四

我在大路的灼热的尘土上消磨了我的白昼。

现在，在黄昏的凉意里，我敲旅店的门。旅店荒凉颓败了。

一棵狰狞的阿刹思树，在墙垣的裂缝里伸展着饥饿的抓紧不放的树根。

曾经有过这样的日子：那时候徒步的旅行者，到这儿来洗濯他们疲倦的双脚。

他们在初升的月亮朦胧的光辉里，在院子里铺开了席子，坐下来畅谈远方异域。

他们在早晨神清气爽地醒来：鸟雀使他们愉快，

① incantation
/ˌɪnkæn'teɪʃən/ n. 咒语，
符咒

② rustle /'rʌsl/ v. 发出沙
沙声

③ scorching /'skɔːtʃɪŋ/
a. 极热的

④ clutch /klʌtʃ/ v. 抓住，
紧紧抓住

⑤ fissure /'fɪʃə/ v. 裂开

The black **smudges**[1] of smoke left by many a forgotten evening lamp stare, like blind eyes, from the wall.

Fireflies flit in the bush near the dried-up pond, and bamboo branches fling their shadows on the grass-grown path.

I am the guest of no one at the end of my day.

The long night is before me, and I am tired.

66

A wandering madman was seeking the touchstone, with matted locks, **tawny**[2] and dust-laden, and body worn to a shadow, his lips tight-pressed, like the shut-up doors of his heart, his burning eyes like the lamp of a glow-worm seeking its mate.

Before him the endless ocean **roared**[3].

The **garrulous**[4] waves ceaselessly talked of hidden treasures, **mocking**[5] the ignorance that knew not their meaning.

Maybe he now had no hope remaining, yet he would not rest, for the search had become his life,—

Just as the ocean for ever lifts its arms to the sky for the unattainable—

Just as the stars go in circles, yet seeking a goal that can never be reached—

Even so on the lonely shore the madman with dusty tawny locks still **roamed**[6] in search of the touchstone.

One day a village boy came up and asked, "Tell me, where did you come at this golden chain about your waist?"

The madman started—the chain that once was iron was verily gold; it was not a dream, but he did not know when it had changed.

友好的繁花在路旁向他们点头致意。

但我来到这儿的时候，没有点亮的灯在等我。

好几盏被遗忘了的黄昏的灯，留下了黑色的煤烟；它像盲人的眼睛，从墙上瞪目凝视。

萤火虫在干涸的池边丛莽里飞翔，竹枝把阴影投掷在长满青草的小径上。

我是在我的白昼尽头、根本没有主人的来客。

漫漫长夜在我的前面，而我是疲倦了。

六六

一个流浪的疯子在寻找点金石，他沾满尘土的头发蓬乱蜡黄，身体消瘦得成了影子。他的嘴唇紧闭，像他紧闭的心扉；而他燃烧着的眼睛，好像是找寻伴侣的萤火虫。

无边的大海在他面前咆哮。

滔滔的波浪不绝地谈到潜藏的宝库，嘲笑那不知其意的人们的愚昧。

也许他现在是一点希望也没有了，然而他不肯罢休，因为这种探索已经成为他的生命，——

正如海洋为了那不可企及的——，永远向天空举起它的胳膊

正如星星周而复始的运行，然而始终追求着永远不能达到的目标——

头发蓬乱蜡黄的疯子竟依旧徘徊在孤寂的海滩上找寻点金石。

有一天，一个村里孩子跑过来问道，"告诉我，你是在哪儿找到那系在你腰间的金链子的？"

---

① smudge /smʌdʒ/ n. 污点,污迹,污斑

② tawny /'tɔːnɪ/ a. 黄褐色的

③ roar /rɔ/ v. 咆哮,怒吼

④ garrulous /'gærʊləs/ a. 话多的;喜欢讲话的

⑤ mock /mɔk/ v. 愚弄,嘲弄

⑥ roam /rəʊm/ v. 随便走,漫步,漫游

He struck his forehead wildly—where, O where had he without knowing it achieved success?

It had grown into a habit, to pick up pebbles and touch the chain, and to throw them away without looking to see if a change had come; thus the madman found and lost the touchstone.

The sun was sinking low in the west, the sky was of gold.

The madman returned on his footsteps to seek anew the lost treasure, with his strength gone, his body bent, and his heart in the dust, like a tree **uprooted**[①].

<h2 style="text-align:center">68</h2>

None lives for ever, brother, and nothing lasts for long. Keep that in mind and **rejoice**[②].

Our life is not the one old burden, our path is not the one long journey.

One sole poet has not to sing one aged song.

The flower fades and dies; but he who wears the flower has not to **mourn**[③] for it for ever.

Brother, keep that in mind and rejoice.

There must come a full pause to weave perfection into music.

Life droops toward its sunset to be drowned in the golden shadows.

Love must be called from its play to drink sorrow and be borne to the heaven of tears.

Brother, keep that in mind and rejoice.

We hasten to gather our flowers lest they are **plundered**[④] by the passing winds.

It quickens our blood and brightens our eyes to snatch kisses that

疯子大吃一惊——过去一度是铁的链子现在确实是金的了；这不是梦，然而他不知道链子在什么时候起的变化。

他狂乱地拍打他的额角——哪儿，啊，他在哪儿不知其然而然地获得了成功？

已经成为一种习惯了，捡起石子，碰一碰链子，然后又把石子掷掉，也不看看是否已经发生变化；疯子就是这样找到了而又失掉了点金石。

太阳正低低地向西方沉落，天空是金色的。

疯子走上回头路，重新去找寻失掉了的宝贝，筋疲力尽，弯腰曲背，心灰意懒，像一棵连根拔起的树木。

六八

没有一个人长生不老，也没有一件东西永久长存。兄弟，记住这一点来欢欣鼓舞吧。

我们的一生不是一个古老的负担，我们的道路不是一条漫长的旅程。

一个独特的诗人不必唱一个古老的歌。

花褪色了凋零了；戴花的人却不必永远为它悲伤。

兄弟，记住这一点来欢欣鼓舞吧。

为了编织完美的音乐，必定要有完全的休止。

为了沉溺在金色的阴影里，人生向夕阳沉落。

必定要把爱从嬉戏中唤回，让它饮下烦恼的酒，把它带到眼泪的天堂。

兄弟，记住这一点来欢欣鼓舞吧。

我们赶紧采集繁花，否则繁花要被路过的风蹂躏了。

① uproot /ʌpˈrʊt/ v. 把(某物)连根拔起;根除

② rejoice /rɪˈdʒɔɪs/ v. 非常高兴;深感欣喜

③ mourn /mɔːn/ v. 哀悼

④ plunder /ˈplʌndə(r)/ v. 劫掠,掠夺

would vanish if we delayed.

Our life is eager, our desires are keen, for time tolls the bell of parting.

Brother, keep that in mind and rejoice.

There is not time for us to clasp a thing and crush it and fling it away to the dust.

The hours trip rapidly away, hiding their dreams in their skirts.

Our life is short; it **yields**[1] but a few days for love.

Were it for work and **drudgery**[2] it would be endlessly long.

Brother, keep that in mind and rejoice.

Beauty is sweet to us, because she dances to the same fleeting tune with our lives.

Knowledge is precious to us, because we shall never have time to complete it.

All is done and finished in the eternal Heaven.

But earth's flowers of illusion are kept eternally fresh by death.

Brother, keep that in mind and rejoice.

72

With days of hard travail I raised a temple. It had no doors or windows, its walls were thickly built with massive stones.

I forgot all else, I shunned all the world, I gazed in rapt **contemplation**[3] at the image I had set upon the altar.

It was always night inside, and lit by the lamps of perfumed oil.

The ceaseless smoke of **incense**[4] wound my heart in its heavy coils.

Sleepless, I **carved**[5] on the walls fantastic figures in mazy bewildering lines—winged horses, flowers with human faces, woman

攫取那迟一步就会消失的吻，使我们的血行迅速，眼睛明亮。

我们的生活是热烈的，我们的欲望是强烈的，因为时间在敲着别离的丧钟。

兄弟，记住这一点来欢欣鼓舞吧。

我们来不及把一件东西抓住，挤碎，而又弃之于尘土。

一个个的时辰，把自己的梦藏在裙子里，迅速地消逝了。

我们的一生是短促的；一生只给我们几天爱的日子。

如果生命是为了艰辛劳役的话，那就无穷地长了。

兄弟，记住这一点来欢欣鼓舞吧。

我们觉得美是甜蜜的，因为她同我们的生命依循着同样飞速的调子一起舞蹈。

我们觉得知识是宝贵的，因为我们永远来不及使知识臻于完善。

一切都是在永恒的天堂里做成和完成的。

然而，大地的幻想之花，是由死亡来长葆永新的。

兄弟，记住这一点来欢欣鼓舞吧。

七二

我连日辛苦，造了一座庙。它没有门没有窗，墙是用巨石密密砌成的。

我忘却其他一切，我躲避整个世界，我在狂喜的沉思里凝视我安置在祭坛上的偶像。

庙里面永远是黑夜，又被香油的灯照明。

供香的不断的烟，袅袅缭绕在我的心头。

① yield /ji:ld/ v. 给,给予
② drudgery /'drʌdʒərɪ/ n. 苦工;单调沉闷的工作

③ contemplation /ˌkɒntəm'pleɪʃən/ n. 沉思,冥想;意图,期望
④ incense /'ɪnsens/ n. 香
⑤ carve /kɑːv/ v. 雕刻,刻

with limbs like **serpents**[1].

No passage was left anywhere through which could enter the song of birds, the **murmur**[2] of leaves or hum of the busy village.

The only sound that echoed in its dark dome was that of **incantations**[3] which I chanted.

My mind became keen and still like a pointed flame, my senses **swooned**[4] in ecstasy.

I knew not how time passed till the thunderstone had struck the temple, and a pain stung me through the heart.

The lamp looked pale and ashamed; the carvings on the walls, like chained dreams, stared meaningless in the light as they **fain**[5] hide themselves.

I looked at the image on the altar. I saw it smiling and alive with the living touch of God. The night I had imprisoned had spread its wings and vanished.

73

Infinite wealth is not yours, my patient and **dusky**[6] mother dust!

You toil to fill the mouths of your children, but food is scarce.

The gift of gladness that you have for us is never perfect.

The toys that you make for your children are **fragile**[7].

You cannot satisfy all our hungry hopes, but should I desert you for that?

Your smile which is shadowed with pain is sweet to my eyes.

Your love which knows not fulfillment is dear to my heart.

From your breast you have fed us with life but not immortality, that is why your eyes are ever wakeful.

① serpent /'sə:pənt/ *n.* 蛇，大蛇

② murmur /'mə:mə/ *n.* 低语声

③ incantation /,ɪnkæn'teɪʃən/ *n.* 咒语，符咒

④ swoon /swu:n/ *v.* 昏厥，昏倒

⑤ fain /feɪn/ *ad.* 宁愿

⑥ dusky /'dʌskɪ/ *a.* 忧郁的

⑦ fragile /'frædʒaɪl/ *a.* 纤巧的；精细的；纤巧美丽的

不睡不眠，我用混乱纷杂的线条，在墙上刻画出荒诞不经的画像——插翅的马，人面的花，四肢像蛇的女人。

哪儿也没有通路可以传进鸟的啁啾，叶子的萧萧，忙忙碌碌村庄的喧哗。

唯一的在这黑暗的庙里回响的声音，就是我诵念咒语的声音。

我的心灵变得敏锐而宁静，像猛烈的火焰；我的感觉昏迷在狂喜之中。

直到庙遭雷殛、我痛彻心扉为止，我不知道时间是怎样消逝的。

灯看上去苍白又含羞；墙上的雕刻像是用链子缚住的梦，在亮光中无谓地瞪着眼睛，仿佛很想把自己掩藏。

我瞧瞧祭台上的偶像。我看见偶像在笑，由于神生动的触摸而生气勃勃。我囚禁起来的黑夜已经展翅飞去，消失无踪了。

七三

无限的财富不是你的，我的坚忍又忧郁的大地母亲啊！

你辛勤劳动，使你的儿女可以糊口，然而食物是稀少的。

你作为礼物送给我们的喜悦，永远是残缺的。

你为你儿女所做的玩具，是脆弱易碎的。

你不能满足我们所有的饥渴的希望，难道我就因此而抛弃你吗？

你那蒙上痛苦的阴影的微笑，对于我的眼睛是甜

For ages you are working with colour and song, yet your heaven is not built, but only its sad suggestion.

Over your creations of beauty there is the mist of tears.

I will pour my songs into your **mute**① heart, and my love into your love.

I will worship you with labour.

I have seen your tender face and I love your mournful dust, Mother Earth.

74

In the world's audience hall, the simple **blade**② of grass sits on the same carpet with the sunbeam and the stars of the midnight.

Thus my songs share their seats in the heart of the world with the music of the clouds and forests.

But, you man of riches, your wealth has no part in the simple grandeur of the sun's glad gold and the mellow gleam of the musing moon.

The blessing of the all-embracing sky is not shed upon it.

And when death appears, it pales and withers and crumbles into dust.

80

with a glance of your eyes you could **plunder**③ all the wealth of songs struck from poets' harps, fair woman!

But for their praises you have no ear, therefore I come to praise you.

You could **humble**④ at your feet the proudest heads in the world.

蜜的。

你那无有穷尽的爱，对于我的心是宝贵的。

你曾经在你的胸膛上以生命而不是以不朽哺育我们，这就是为什么你的眼睛永远是惊醒的缘故。

多少年来你以色彩和歌曲工作着，然而你的天堂并没有造成，只造成了伤心的、使人想起天堂的东西。

在你所创造的美丽的东西上面，笼罩着泪水的雾气。

我要以我的歌注入你缄默的心，以我的爱注入你的爱。

我要以劳动来敬奉你。

我看到了你温柔的脸，我热爱你哀伤的尘土，大地母亲啊。

七四

在世界的听众会堂里，朴素的草叶，跟阳光和子夜的星辰同席共谈。

我的歌，就是这样的跟云和森林的音乐一同在世界的心里分占着席位。

朴素庄严的是太阳愉快的金色，是沉思的月亮柔美的光辉；可是你，有钱的人啊，你的财富却与这种朴素庄严无关。

拥抱一切的天空的祝福，是并不落在财富上的。

而当死亡出现的时候，财富就褪色，枯萎，化为尘土了。

八〇

美丽的女人啊，你能以你眼睛的一个流盼，掠尽诗人竖琴上弹奏的歌曲的全部财富！

① mute /mjuːt/ *a.* 缄默的；无声的

② blade /bleɪd/ *n.* 叶片；桨叶

③ plunder /ˈplʌndə (r)/ *v.* 劫掠，掠夺

④ humble /ˈhʌmbl/ *v.* 使谦恭；使卑下

But it is your loved ones, unknown to fame, whom you choose to worship, therefore I worship you.

The perfection of your arms would add glory to kingly splendour with their touch.

But you use them to sweep away the dust, and to make clean your humble home, therefore I am filled with awe.

82

We are to play the game of death to-night, my bride and I.

The night is black, the clouds in the sky are **capricious**[①], and the waves are **raving**[②] at sea.

We have left our bed of dreams, flung open the door and come out, my bride and I.

We sit upon a swing, and the storm winds give us a wild push from behind.

My bride starts up with fear and delight, she trembles and clings to my breast.

Long have I served her tenderly.

I made for her a bed of flowers and I closed the doors to shut out the rude light from her eyes.

I kissed her gently on her lips and whispered softly in her ears till she half swooned in **languor**[③].

She was lost in the endless mist of vague sweetness.

She answered not to my touch, my songs failed to arouse her.

To-night has come to us the call of the storm from the wild.

My bride has **shivered**[④] and stood up, she has clasped my hand and come out.

然而你对诗人的歌颂却充耳不闻，因此我就来歌颂你。

你能使世界上最骄傲的人拜倒在你的脚下。

然而你选以崇拜的，却是你所爱的无名的人，所以我崇拜你。

你那完美的手臂的触摸爱抚，将使帝王的尊荣增加光辉。

然而你却用以扫除尘土，清洁你朴实无华的家，因此我就满心敬爱你。

八二

今夜，我和我的新娘要玩死亡的游戏。

夜是黑的，天空里的云是变幻莫测的，而海上的波涛正在怒吼。

我和我的新娘，离开了入梦的床，打开大门，走出门来。

我们坐在秋千上，暴风从后面给我们一阵狂野的推动。

我的新娘又喜又惧地跳起身来，战战兢兢，紧紧偎依在我的胸口。

我温柔地侍奉了她好久。

我给她做了个繁花缀成的床，我关上门，不让粗暴的光芒照射她的眼睛。

我轻轻吻她的嘴唇，柔声在她耳边低语，直至她在慵倦中半陷入昏迷。

她迷失在朦胧的甜情蜜意的无穷迷雾里。

她不回答我手的爱抚，而我的歌也唤不醒她。

今夜旷野风暴的呼唤，传到了我们的耳边。

① capricious /kə'prɪʃəs/ a. 变幻莫测的

② rave /reɪv/ v. 呼啸，咆哮，怒号

③ languor /'læŋgə/ n. 无精打采

④ shiver /'ʃɪvə/ v.（因寒冷，害怕等）颤抖，哆嗦

Her hair is flying in the wind, her veil is fluttering, her **garland**[1] rustles over her breast.

The push of death has swung her into life.

We are face to face and heart to heart, my bride and I.

83

She dwelt on the hillside by the edge of a maize-field, near the spring that flows in laughing rills through the **solemn**[2] shadows of ancient trees. The women came there to fill their jars, and travellers would sit there to rest and talk. She worked and dreamed daily to the tune of the bubbling stream.

One evening the stranger came down from the cloud-hidden peak; his locks were tangled like **drowsy**[3] snakes. We asked in wonder, "Who are you?" He answered not but sat by the garrulous stream and silently gazed at the hut where she dwelt. Our hearts quaked in fear and we came back home when it was night.

Next morning when the women came to fetch water at the spring by the deodar trees, they found the doors open in her hut, but her voice was gone and where was her smiling face? The empty jar lay on the floor and her lamp had burnt itself out in the corner. No one knew where she had fled to before it was morning—and the stranger had gone.

In the month of May the sun grew strong and the snow melted, and we sat by the spring and wept. We wondered in our mind, "Is there a spring in the land where she has gone and where she can fill her vessel in these hot thirsty days?" And we asked each other in **dismay**[4], "Is there a land beyond these hills where we live?"

It was a summer night; the breeze blew from the south; and I sat in

① garland /'gɑːlənd/ n. 花环;花冠;花圈

② solemn /'sɔləm/ a. 冷峻的,表情严肃的

③ drowsy /'drauzɪ/ a. 欲睡的,半睡的,昏昏欲睡的

④ dismay /dis'meɪ/ n. 诧异,惊愕

我的新娘战栗,站起身来,她抓住了我的手跑出去。

她的头发在风中飞舞,她的面纱飘扬,她的花环在她胸口飒飒作响。

死亡的推动——把她推进了生的境界。

我和我的新娘,我们脸对着脸、心对着心。

八三

她住在玉米田边的山麓,在那化作哗笑的小溪、流过古树的庄严阴影的泉边。妇人们到那儿去盛满她们的水壶,旅人们常坐在那儿休息谈天。她每天伴随着溪声潺潺,工作和做梦。

一天黄昏,陌生人从白雪深处的山峰上下来;陌生人的头发纠结如困倦的蛇。我们诧异地问:"你是谁?"他不回答,却坐在潺潺不息的溪畔,默默地凝望她所住的茅屋。我们的心在恐惧中发抖,我们回家时天已经黑了。

第二天,妇人们到雪松旁的泉水边取水,她们发现她的茅屋门户洞开,然而她的声音是没有了,她微笑的脸又在哪儿呢?空空的水壶倒在地板上,她的油灯已经在角落里燃尽了。没有人知道她在天亮以前跑到哪儿去了——而陌生人已经走了。

在五月这一个月里,太阳强烈起来了,雪融了,可我们坐在泉水边哭泣。我们心里诧异:"她所去的地方可有泉水,她能在这些炎热口渴的日子里盛满她的水壶吗?"我们互相惊异地询问:"在我们所居住的这些山岭外面,可有陆地吗?"

her deserted room where the lamp stood still unlit. When suddenly from before my eyes the hills vanished like curtains drawn aside. "Ah, it is she who comes. How are you, my child? Are you happy? But where can you shelter under this open sky? And, **alas**①, our spring is not here to **allay**② your thirst."

"Here is the same sky, "she said, "only free from the fencing hills, — this is the same stream grown into a plain." "Everything is here, "I sighed, "only we are not." She smiled sadly and said, "You are in my heart." I woke up and heard the babbling of the stream and the rustling of the deodars at night.

85

Who are you, reader, reading my poems an hundred years hence?

I cannot send you one single flower from this wealth of the spring, one single streak of gold from yonder clouds.

Open your doors and look abroad.

From your blossoming garden gather fragrant memories of the vanished flowers of an hundred years before.

In the joy of your heart may you feel the living joy that sang one spring morning, sending its glad voice across an hundred years.

是夏夜，微风从南方吹来；我坐在她的寂无人影的房间里，灯摆在那儿，依旧没有点上。突然，山岭在我眼前消失了，仿佛是拉开的幕布。"啊，原来是她来了。你好吗，我的孩子？你幸福吗？可是，在这露天之下，你能在何处藏身呢？咳，可惜我们的泉水不在这儿，不能解你的渴。"

"这儿是同样的天空，"她说，"只是没有山岭的屏障罢了——扩大成为河的就是那同一条溪水，展开成为平原的就是那同一个大地。""这儿一切俱全，"我叹息道，"只是我们可不在这儿啊。"她悲哀地微笑，说道，"你们在我的心里。"我醒来，听到了夜间溪声潺潺，雪松萧萧。

八五

一百年后读着我的诗篇的读者啊，你是谁呢？

我不能从这春天的富丽里送你一朵花，我不能从那边的云彩里送你一缕金霞。

打开你的门眺望吧。

从你那繁花盛开的花园里，收集百年前消逝的花朵的芬芳馥郁的记忆吧。

在你心头的欢乐里，愿你能感觉到某一个春天早晨歌唱过的、那生气勃勃的欢乐，越过一百年传来它愉快的歌声。

① alas /ə'læs/ *int.* （表示悲痛、遗憾）哎呀！
② allay /ə'leɪ/ *v.* 减轻，缓和

Gitanjali

吉檀迦利

1

Thou hast made me endless, such is thy pleasure. This **frail**[①] vessel thou emptiest again and again, and fillest it ever with fresh life.

This little flute of a reed thou hast carried over hills and **dales**[②], and hast breathed through it melodies eternally new.

At the immortal touch of thy hands my little heart loses its limits in joy and gives birth to utterance **ineffable**[③].

Thy infinite gifts come to me only on these very small hands of mine. Ages pass, and still thou pourest, and still there is room to fill.

2

When thou commandest me to sing it seems that my heart would break with pride; and I look to thy face, and tears come to my eyes.

All that is harsh and **dissonant**[④] in my life **melts**[⑤] into one sweet harmony — and my adoration spreads wings like a glad bird on its flight across the sea.

I know thou takest pleasure in my singing. I know that only as a singer I come before thy presence.

I touch by the edge of the far-spreading wing of my song thy feet which I could never aspire to reach.

Drunk with the joy of singing I forget myself and call thee friend who art my lord.

4

Life of my life, I shall ever try to keep my body pure, knowing that thy living touch is upon all my limbs.

I shall ever try to keep all untruths out from my thoughts, knowing

① frail /freɪl/ *a.* 脆弱的，易损坏的
② dale /deɪl/ *n.* 〈诗〉谷，峪

③ ineffable /ɪnˈefəbl/ *a.* 言语无法表达的，不可言喻的

④ dissonant /ˈdɪsənənt/ *a.* 不和谐的，刺耳的
⑤ melt /melt/ *v.* （使）融化；溶解

一

你已经使我臻于无穷无尽的境界，你乐于如此。这薄而脆的酒杯，你再三地饮尽，总是重新斟满新的生命。

你翻过山岭、越过溪谷带来这小小芦笛，用它吹出永远新鲜的曲调。

在你双手不朽的安抚下，我小小的心里乐无止境，发出的乐声亦非笔墨所能形容。

你无穷的赐予只送到我这双小之又小的手里。许多时代消逝了，你的赐予依旧在倾注，而我的手里还有余地可以充满。

二

你命令我歌唱的时候，我自豪，似乎心都快爆裂了；我凝望你的脸，泪水涌到我的眼睛里。

我生命里一切刺耳的与不悦耳的，都融成一片甜美的和谐音乐——而我的崇拜敬慕之情，像一只快乐的鸟儿，展翅翱翔，飞越海洋。

我知道你喜欢听我唱歌。我知道我只有作为歌手才能来到你的面前。

我用我歌儿的庞大翅膀的边缘，轻拂着你的双脚——那可是我从不奢望企及的。

我陶醉于歌唱的欢乐，忘乎所以，你明明是我的主，我却称你为朋友。

四

我生命的生命啊，知道你生气勃勃的爱抚抚在我的四肢上，我一定努力使我的躯体永远保持纯洁。

知道你就是点亮了我心灵里的理智之灯的真理，

that thou art that truth which has kindled the light of reason in my mind.

I shall ever try to drive all evils away from my heart and keep my love in flower, knowing that thou hast thy seat in the inmost **shrine**[①] of my heart.

And it shall be my endeavour to reveal thee in my actions, knowing it is thy power gives me strength to act.

6

Pluck this little flower and take it, delay not! I fear lest it **droop**[②] and drop into the dust.

I may not find a place in thy garland, but honour it with a touch of pain from thy hand and pluck it. I fear lest the day end before I am aware, and the time of offering go by.

Though its colour be not deep and its smell be **faint**[③], use this flower in thy service and pluck it while there is time.

7

My song has put off her **adornments**[④]. She has no pride of dress and decoration. Ornaments would **mar**[⑤] our union; they would come between thee and me; their jingling would drown thy whispers.

My poet's vanity dies in shame before thy sight. O master poet, I have sat down at thy feet. Only let me make my life simple and straight, like a flute of reed for thee to fill with music.

8

The child who is decked with prince's robes and who has jewelled chains round his neck loses all pleasure in his play; his dress **hampers**[⑥]

我一定努力把一切虚伪从我的思想里永远排除。

知道你在我内心的圣殿里安置了你的座位，我一定努力把一切邪恶从我的心里永远驱除，并且使我的爱情永远开花。

知道是你的神威给我以行动的力量，我一定努力在我的行动中将你体现。

六

摘下这朵小花，拿走吧。别迁延时日了！我担心花会凋谢，落入尘土。

也许这小花不配放进你的花环，但还是摘下它，以你的手的采摘之劳给它以光荣吧。我担心在我不知不觉间白昼已尽，贡献的时辰已经过去了。

虽然这小花颜色不深，香气也是淡淡的，还是及早采摘，用它来礼拜吧。

七

我的诗歌已卸去她的装饰。她已无衣饰豪华的骄傲。装饰品会损害我们的结合；装饰品会阻隔在你与我之间；环佩叮当的声音会淹没你的柔声细语。

我诗人的虚荣，在你面前羞惭地化为乌有。诗歌的宗师啊，我已经坐在你的足下。但愿我的生活单纯正直，像一支芦笛，供你奏乐。

八

给孩子穿上王子的衣袍，脖子上又挂上珠宝项链，他在游戏中便失去了一切乐趣；他的衣饰步步都阻碍

① shrine /ʃraɪn/ *n.* 圣坛；神圣场所

② droop /druːp/ *v.* (植物等)萎垂

③ faint /feɪnt/ *a.* 微弱的

④ adornment /əˈdɔːnmənt/ *n.* 装饰
⑤ mar /maː/ *v.* 损坏，损害

⑥ hamper /ˈhæmpə(r)/ *v.* 妨碍，阻碍

him at every step.

In fear that it may be **frayed**[1], or stained with dust he keeps himself from the world, and is afraid even to move.

Mother, it is no gain, thy bondage of **finery**[2], if it keeps one shut off from the healthful dust of the earth, if it rob one of the right of entrance to the great fair of common human life.

10

Here is thy footstool and there rest thy feet where live the poorest, and lowliest, and lost.

When I try to bow to thee, my obeisance cannot reach down to the depth where thy feet rest among the poorest, and lowliest, and lost.

Pride can never approach to where thou walkest in the clothes of the humble among the poorest, and lowliest, and lost.

My heart can never find its way to where thou keepest company with the companionless among the poorest, the lowliest, and the lost.

11

Leave this chanting and singing and telling of beads! Whom dost thou worship in this lonely dark corner of a temple with doors all shut? Open thine eyes and see thy God is not before thee!

He is there where the **tiller**[3] is tilling the hard ground and where the pathmaker is breaking stones. He is with them in sun and in shower, and his garment is covered with dust. Put off thy holy mantle and even like him come down on the dusty soil!

Deliverance? Where is this deliverance to be found? Our master himself has joyfully taken upon him the bonds of creation; he is bound

着他。

生怕衣饰被磨损或被尘土玷污，他总是回避这个世界，甚至连动一动也忧心忡忡。

母亲啊，华服盛装的约束，如果它使人和大地健康的尘土隔绝，如果它剥夺人进入人类日常生活盛大庙会的权利，那就不是得而是失了。

一〇

这是你的脚凳；最贫贱最潦倒的人们生活的地方，便是你歇足之处。

你歇脚在最贫贱、最潦倒的人们中间，我竭力向你鞠躬致意，可我的敬意达不到个中深处。

你穿着寒酸的衣服，行走在最贫贱、最潦倒的人们中间，骄傲可永远到不了这个地方。

你同最贫贱、最潦倒的人们之中那些没有同伴的人做伴，我的心可永远找不到通向那儿的道路。

一一

别再诵经、唱经和数珠吧！在这重门紧闭的庙宇的幽暗寂寞的角落里，你在礼拜谁呢？睁开眼睛瞧瞧，你的神可不在你的面前！

神在农民翻耕坚硬泥土的地方，在筑路工人敲碎石子的地方。炎阳下，阵雨里，神都和他们同在，神的袍子上蒙着尘土。脱下你的圣袍，甚至像神一样到尘埃飞扬的泥土这里来吧！

解脱？哪儿找得到这种解脱？我们的主亲自欢欢喜喜地承担了创造世界的责任；他就得永远和我们大

① fray /freɪ/ v. 使磨损

② finery /'faɪnərɪ/ n. 华丽、优雅的服装

③ tiller /'tɪlə/ n. 耕者，农夫

with us all for ever.

Come out of thy meditations and leave aside thy flowers and incense! What harm is there if thy clothes become **tattered** [1] and stained? Meet him and stand by him in toil and in sweat of thy brow.

12

The time that my journey takes is long and the way of it long.

I came out on the chariot of the first gleam of light, and pursued my voyage through the wildernesses of worlds leaving my track on many a star and planet.

It is the most distant course that comes nearest to thyself, and that training is the most intricate which leads to the utter simplicity of a tune.

The traveller has to knock at every alien door to come to his own, and one has to wander through all the outer worlds to reach the innermost shrine at the end.

My eyes strayed far and wide before I shut them and said 'Here art thou!'

The question and the cry 'Oh, where?' melt into tears of a thousand streams and **deluge** [2] the world with the flood of the assurance 'I am!'

13

The song that I came to sing remains unsung to this day.

I have spent my days in stringing and in unstringing my instrument.

The time has not come true, the words have not been rightly set; only there is the agony of wishing in my heart.

The blossom has not opened; only the wind is sighing by.

家在一起。

丢掉你的鲜花和焚香，从你的静坐沉思里走出来吧。如果你的衣衫褴褛而肮脏，那又何妨呢？在辛勤劳动中流着额上的汗，去迎接神，同神站在一起吧。

一二

我跋涉的时间是漫长的，跋涉的道路也是漫长的。

我出门坐上第一道晨光的车子，奔驰于大千世界的茫茫旷野里，在许多恒星和行星上留下了我的踪迹。

到达离你自己最近的地方，路途最为遥远；达到音调单纯朴素的极境，经过的训练最为复杂艰巨。

旅人叩过了每一个陌生人家的门，才来到他自己的家门口；人要踏遍外边大千世界，临了才到达藏得最深的圣殿。

我的眼睛找遍了四面八方，我才合上眼睛，说道："原来你在这儿！"

这问题和这呼喊，"啊，在哪儿呢？"融成了千条泪水的川流，然后才和"我在这儿！"这保证的洪流，一同泛滥于全世界。

一三

我想唱的歌，直到今天依旧没有唱出来。

我把日子都花在调弄乐器的弦索上了。

节奏还不合拍，歌词还没配妥；我心里只有渴望的痛苦。

鲜花还没有开放，只有风在旁边唏嘘而过。

我不曾见到他的脸，也不曾听到他说话的声音；

① tattered /'tætəd/ *a.* 破烂的,褴褛的

② deluge /'delju:dʒ/ *v.* 泛滥

I have not seen his face, nor have I listened to his voice; only I have heard his gentle footsteps from the road before my house.

The livelong day has passed in spreading his seat on the floor; but the lamp has not been lit and I cannot ask him into my house.

I live in the hope of meeting with him; but this meeting is not yet.

18

Clouds heap upon clouds and it darkens. Ah, love, why dost thou let me wait outside at the door all alone?

In the busy moments of the noontide work I am with the crowd, but on this dark lonely day it is only for thee that I hope.

If thou showest me not thy face, if thou leavest me wholly aside, I know not how I am to pass these long, rainy hours.

I keep gazing on the far-away gloom of the sky, and my heart wanders wailing with the restless wind.

19

If thou speakest not I will fill my heart with thy silence and endure it. I will keep still and wait like the night with starry **vigil**[①] and its head bent low with patience.

The morning will surely come, the darkness will vanish, and thy voice pour down in golden streams breaking through the sky.

Then thy words will take wing in songs from every one of my birds' nests, and thy melodies will break forth in flowers in all my forest groves.

我只听见他轻轻的脚步声，在我房子前面的大路上走
过。

漫长的一天都消磨在为他在地上铺设座位了，而灯
却还没有点亮，我还不能请他进屋来。

我生活在同他相见的希望里；然而这相见的时机
尚未到来。

一八

云霾重重堆积，天色暗下来了。啊，我爱，你为
什么让我孤零零地在门外等候？

在中午工作忙碌的时刻里，我和大伙儿在一起，
但在这暗淡寂寞的日子里，我希望的只是和你在一起。

如果你不让我看到你的容颜，如果你完全把我抛
开，我就不知道怎样度过这些漫长下雨的时辰。

我始终凝望着天空遥远的阴霾，我的心和不安宁
的风一同踯躅哀号。

一九

如果你不说话，我就忍耐着，以你的沉默充实我
的心。我一定保持沉静，像黑夜，在繁星闪烁下通宵
无眠地等待，耐心地俯首低身。

早晨一定会到来，黑暗一定会消失，而你的声音
一定会划破长空，在金色河流中倾泻而下。

这时你说的话，都会在我的每一个小鸟巢里变成
歌曲，振翅飞翔，而你的音乐，也会在我的所有丛林
中盛放繁花。

① vigil /'vɪdʒɪl/ n. 不眠，失眠

20

On the day when the lotus bloomed, alas, my mind was straying, and I knew it not. My basket was empty and the flower remained unheeded.

Only now and again a sadness fell upon me, and I started up from my dream and felt a sweet trace of a strange fragrance in the south wind.

That vague sweetness made my heart ache with longing and it seemed to me that was the eager breath of the summer seeking for its completion.

I knew not then that it was so near, that it was mine, and that this perfect sweetness had blossomed in the depth of my own heart.

21

I must launch out my boat. The **languid**[①] hours pass by on the shore — Alas for me!

The spring has done its flowering and taken leave. And now with the burden of faded futile flowers I wait and linger.

The waves have become clamorous, and upon the bank in the shady lane the yellow leaves flutter and fall.

What emptiness do you gaze upon! Do you not feel a thrill passing through the air with the notes of the far-away song floating from the other shore?

23

Art thou abroad on this stormy night on thy journey of love, my friend? The sky groans like one in despair.

I have no sleep tonight. Ever and again I open my door and look out

二〇

莲花盛开的那一天，唉，我心不在焉，而我自己却不知不觉。我的花篮里空空如也，而我对鲜花可依旧视而不见。

不时有一股哀愁袭来，我从梦中惊起，觉得南风里有一缕奇香的芳踪。

这朦胧的温柔之情，使我的心因思慕而疼痛，我觉得这好比夏天热烈的气息在寻求其圆满的境界。

那时我不知道，这完美的温柔之情，竟是那么近，竟是我自己的，而且已经在我自己的内心深处开花了。

二一

我必须把船开出去了。可惜啊，我意兴阑珊的光阴在岸边虚度了！

春天开过花就告辞了。而今背负着落花狼藉的包袱，我却等待而又流连。

涛声喧哗，岸上树荫小巷里黄叶飘零。

你凝望的是何等空虚，你可感觉到，随着从彼岸飘扬过来的歌声，自有一种惊喜之情流贯天空？

二三

是你在这暴风雨之夜，在你那爱的旅途上跋涉，我的朋友？天空，像个失望的人在呻吟哀号。

我今夜无眠。我再三打开大门，向门外黑暗中张望，我的朋友！

我眼前什么也看不见，我不知道你走的道路在哪儿。

① languid /'læŋgwɪd/ *a.* 无精打采的

on the darkness, my friend!

I can see nothing before me. I wonder where lies thy path!

By what dim shore of the ink-black river, by what far edge of the frowning forest, through what mazy depth of gloom art thou threading thy course to come to me, my friend?

26

He came and sat by my side but I woke not. What a cursed sleep it was, O miserable me!

He came when the night was still; he had his harp in his hands, and my dreams became **resonant**[1] with its melodies.

Alas, why are my nights all thus lost? Ah, why do I ever miss his sight whose breath touches my sleep?

29

He whom I enclose with my name is weeping in this dungeon. I am ever busy building this wall all around; and as this wall goes up into the sky day by day I lose sight of my true being in its dark shadow.

I take pride in this great wall, and I **plaster**[2] it with dust and sand lest a least hole should be left in this name; and for all the care I take I lose sight of my true being.

30

I came out alone on my way to my **tryst**[3]. But who is this that follows me in the silent dark?

I move aside to avoid his presence but I escape him not.

是你从那墨黑河流的昏暗岸边，经过颦眉蹙额的森林边缘，穿过幽暗深处的迷津，迂回曲折地来到我的身边，我的朋友？

二六

他来坐在我的身边，我却浓睡未醒。好一个可咒诅的睡眠，唉，不幸的我！

他来的时候，夜是静悄悄的；他手里拿着竖琴，我做的梦同他奏的乐共振共鸣。

唉，为什么我的良宵全都这样虚度了？啊，他的气息触及了我的睡眠，为什么我总是见不到他呢？

二九

我用我的"名"把他圈禁起来，而他在这监狱里哭泣。我总是忙于在周围筑墙；墙垣一天天高入云霄，我就看不见在黑沉沉阴影里的真我了。

我以这伟大的城垣自豪，我用泥和沙抹墙，生怕我这"名"之墙上还有一星半点的漏洞；尽管我煞费苦心，我可看不见真我了。

三〇

我独自上路，去赴我的约会。可这在寂静的黑暗中跟着我的是谁呢？

我靠边走，躲开他，然而我摆脱不了他。

他昂首阔步，扬起地上的尘埃；我每说一句话，

① resonant /'rezənənt/ *a.* 引起共鸣的

② plaster /'plɑːstə/ *v.* 在…上抹灰泥，厚厚地涂抹

③ tryst /trɪst/ *n.* （情人的）约会，幽会

He makes the dust rise from the earth with his swagger; he adds his loud voice to every word that I utter.

He is my own little self, my lord, he knows no shame; but I am ashamed to come to thy door in his company.

35

Where the mind is without fear and the head is held high;

Where knowledge is free;

Where the world has not been broken up into fragments by narrow domestic walls;

Where words come out from the depth of truth;

Where tireless striving stretches its arms towards perfection;

Where the clear stream of reason has not lost its way into the **dreary**[①] desert sand of dead habit;

Where the mind is led forward by thee into ever-widening thought and action —

Into that heaven of freedom, my Father, let my country awake.

37

I thought that my voyage had come to its end at the last limit of my power, — that the path before me was closed, that provisions were exhausted and the time come to take shelter in a silent obscurity.

But I find that thy will knows no end in me. And when old words die out on the tongue, new melodies break forth from the heart; and where the old tracks are lost, new country is revealed with its wonders.

他都添上他的大叫大嚷。

他是我自己的小我，我的主啊，他不识羞耻；然而我却羞于和他一同来到你的门口。

三五

在那儿，心灵是无畏的，头是昂得高高的；

在那儿，知识是自由自在的；

在那儿，世界不曾被狭小家宅的墙垣分割成一块块的；

在那儿，话语来自真理深处；

在那儿，不倦的努力把胳膊伸向完美；

在那儿，理智的清流不曾迷失在积习的荒凉沙漠里；

在那儿，心灵受你指引，走向日益开阔的思想和行动——

我的父啊，让我的国家觉醒，进入那自由的天堂吧！

三七

我以为我的旅程已经终结，我的力量已经枯竭，我的前途已经断绝，我的粮食已经耗尽——我托庇于寂静、混沌的大限，已经到来了。

然而我发现，你的意志在我身上不知有终点。旧的言语刚在舌尖上消失，新的乐曲又从心上迸发而出；旧的车辙消失了，新的田野又显示出奇观来了。

① dreary /ˈdrɪərɪ/ a. 枯燥无味，单调的

41

Where dost thou stand behind them all, my lover, hiding thyself in the shadows? They push thee and pass thee by on the dusty road, taking thee for **naught**[1]. I wait here weary hours spreading my offerings for thee, while passers-by come and take my flowers, one by one, and my basket is nearly empty.

The morning time is past, and the noon. In the shade of evening my eyes are drowsy with sleep. Men going home glance at me and smile and fill me with shame. I sit like a beggar maid, drawing my skirt over my face, and when they ask me, what it is I want, I drop my eyes and answer them not.

Oh, how, indeed, could I tell them that for thee I wait, and that thou hast promised to come. How could I utter for shame that I keep for my **dowry**[2] this poverty. Ah, I hug this pride in the secret of my heart.

I sit on the grass and gaze upon the sky and dream of the sudden splendour of thy coming — all the lights ablaze, golden **pennons**[3] flying over thy car, and they at the roadside standing **agape**[4], when they see thee come down from thy seat to raise me from the dust, and set at thy side this ragged beggar girl a-tremble with shame and pride, like a creeper in a summer breeze.

But time glides on and still no sound of the wheels of thy chariot. Many a procession passes by with noise and shouts and glamour of glory. Is it only thou who wouldst stand in the shadow silent and behind them all? And only I who would wait and weep and wear out my heart in vain longing?

四一

　　我的爱人，你，站在他们的背后，藏身在阴影里，你究竟在何处呢？在尘土飞扬的道路上，他们推开你，走了过去，把你漠视。我在这儿摆上我的礼物，长时间地等候你，等得人都倦了；而过路的人来了，一朵又一朵地取走我的花儿，我的花篮几乎是空空的了。

　　早晨过去了，中午也过去了。在黄昏的朦胧里，我的眼睛困倦欲睡。回家的人们，带着微笑瞧我，使我满心羞惭。我像个女丐一样坐着，拉起一角裙子遮住我的脸，他们问我可要什么的时候，我垂首低眉不语。

　　啊，真的，我怎么能告诉他们：我是在等候你，而且你已经答允我要来的呢？我又怎么能惭愧地说，我留着这份贫穷作为陪嫁呢？啊，我在内心的秘密深处拥抱着这种自豪感。

　　我坐在草地上凝望天空，梦想着你降临时突如其来的豪华壮观——万道光芒熠熠生辉，金色的旗帜在你车辇上飘扬，而他们站在道旁张大着嘴巴，眼看着你从车辇的座位上走将下来，把我从尘埃中扶了起来，把我这衣衫褴褛的女丐坐在你的身旁，我又羞惭又自豪，浑身颤抖，像是夏天习习凉风里的一支藤蔓。

　　然而，时间流逝，依旧听不见你车辇的轮声。许多仪仗队，喧哗、显赫地走过去了。只有你宁可站在他们大家的背后、悄悄地藏身在阴影里？只有我宁可等待、哭泣，在徒然的朝思暮想中磨碎我的心？

① naught /nɔːt/ n. 没有什么;无;不存在

② dowry /'dauərɪ/ n. 嫁妆

③ pennon /'penən/ n. 旗帜

④ agape /ə'geɪp/ ad. （因惊奇等）大张着嘴的

42

Early in the day it was whispered that we should sail in a boat, only thou and I, and never a soul in the world would know of this our pilgrimage to no country and to no end.

In that shoreless ocean, at thy silently listening smile my songs would swell in melodies, free as waves, free from all bondage of words.

Is the time not come yet? Are there works still to do? Lo, the evening has come down upon the shore and in the fading light the seabirds come flying to their nests.

Who knows when the chains will be off, and the boat, like the last glimmer of sunset, vanish into the night?

43

The day was when I did not keep myself in readiness for thee; and entering my heart unbidden even as one of the common crowd, unknown to me, my king, thou didst press the **signet**[①] of eternity upon many a fleeting moment of my life.

And today when by chance I light upon them and see thy signature, I find they have lain scattered in the dust mixed with the memory of joys and sorrows of my trivial days forgotten.

Thou didst not turn in contempt from my childish play among dust, and the steps that I heard in my playroom are the same that are echoing from star to star.

47

The night is nearly spent waiting for him in vain. I fear lest in the morning he suddenly come to my door when I have fallen asleep wearied

四二

清晨密语，说是我们，只有你和我要驾起一叶扁舟，世界上没有一个人会知道我们这没有目的地也没有穷尽的遨游。

在无涯无际的海洋上，在你微笑静听之际，我会放声歌唱，曲调抑扬低昂，摆脱字句的束缚，自由如波浪翻腾。

时辰还没有到吗？还有工作要做吗？瞧啊，黄昏已经笼罩海岸，苍茫暮色里海鸟正在归巢。

谁知道什么时候将解开链索，这一叶扁舟会像落日的余光，消失在黑夜之中呢？

四三

那天我没有准备迎接你；我的国王，你就像一个素昧平生的普通人，自动进入我的心扉，你在我一生不少飞逝的流光里，盖上了永生的印章。

今天我偶然照亮了飞逝的流光，看到了你的印章，我发现它们同我遗忘了的、无足轻重的往日的有苦有乐的回忆混杂在一起，散乱地撒在尘土里。

你对我在尘土里的童稚游戏并不鄙夷掉头不顾，我在游戏室里听到的足音，便是在繁星之间回响着的足音。

① signet /'sɪgnɪt/ *n.* 印章

四七

夜阑了，白白地等候他了。我生怕他在清晨突然来到门口，而我却疲倦得睡熟了。啊，朋友们，别挡驾，让他通行无阻吧。

out. Oh friends, leave the way open to him — forbid him not.

If the sounds of his steps does not wake me, do not try to **rouse**[1] me, I pray. I wish not to be called from my sleep by the clamorous choir of birds, by the riot of wind at the festival of morning light. Let me sleep undisturbed even if my lord comes of a sudden to my door.

Ah, my sleep, precious sleep, which only waits for his touch to vanish. Ah, my closed eyes that would open their lids only to the light of his smile when he stands before me like a dream emerging from darkness of sleep.

Let him appear before my sight as the first of all lights and all forms. The first thrill of joy to my awakened soul let it come from his glance. And let my return to myself be immediate return to him.

51

The night darkened. Our day's works had been done. We thought that the last guest had arrived for the night and the doors in the village were all shut. Only some said the king was to come. We laughed and said 'No, it cannot be!'

It seemed there were knocks at the door and we said it was nothing but the wind. We put out the lamps and lay down to sleep. Only some said, 'It is the messenger!' We laughed and said 'No, it must be the wind!'

There came a sound **in the dead of the night**[2]. We sleepily thought it was the distant thunder. The earth shook, the walls rocked, and it troubled us in our sleep. Only some said it was the sound of wheels. We said in a drowsy murmur, 'No, it must be the rumbling of clouds!'

The night was still dark when the drum sounded. The voice came

① rouse /'rauz/ *v.* 唤醒

　　如果他的脚步声没有把我惊醒，请不要设法把我叫醒。我不愿意众鸟嘈杂的合唱、晨光庆典上的大风狂啸，把我从酣睡中吵醒。让我毫无打扰地安睡吧，哪怕是我的主突然来到我的门口。

　　啊，我的睡眠，我的宝贵的睡眠，只等着在他的抚摸下消失。啊，我的紧闭的眼睛，只等着在他的微笑下睁开眼皮，这时候他站在我的眼前，就像一个梦从黑暗的睡眠里浮现。

　　让他作为一切光芒中的第一道光芒，一切形态里的第一个形态，呈现在我的眼前。让我觉醒的灵魂的第一阵惊喜之情，来自他的目光。让我的返归自我，成为直接对他的皈依。

五一

　　夜色黑沉沉的。我们白天的工作已经做完。我们认为今夜最后一个投宿的客人已经来到，村子里家家都已门关户闭。只有几个人说是国王要来的。我们笑笑说："不，这是不可能的！"

　　仿佛有叩门的声音，而我们说这不过是风。我们灭了灯，躺下来睡觉。只有几个人说："这是使者！"我们笑笑，说，"不，这必定是风！"

② in the dead of the night 夜深人静的时候

　　夜深人静时又传来一个声音。我们在朦胧中以为这是遥远的雷声。地动墙摇，扰乱了我们的睡眠。只有几个人说这是车轮的声音。我们睡意正浓地喃喃说道："不，这必定是云霄雷鸣！"

　　响起鼓声时夜还是黑沉沉的，传来了呼喊："醒来吧，别耽误了！"我们双手按住心头，害怕得发抖。

'Wake up! delay not! ' We pressed our hands on our hearts and shuddered with fear. Some said, 'Lo, there is the king's flag! ' We stood up on our feet and cried 'There is no time for delay! '

The king has come — but where are lights, where are wreaths? Where is the throne to seat him? Oh, shame! Oh utter shame! Where is the hall, the decorations? Someone has said, 'Vain is this cry! Greet him with empty hands, lead him into thy rooms all bare! '

Open the doors, let the conch-shells be sounded! In the depth of the night has come the king of our dark, **dreary**[1] house. The thunder roars in the sky. The darkness shudders with lightning. Bring out thy tattered piece of mat and spread it in the courtyard. With the storm has come of a sudden our king of the fearful night.

52

I thought I should ask of thee — but I dared not — the rose wreath thou hadst on thy neck. Thus I waited for the morning, when thou didst depart, to find a few fragments on the bed. And like a beggar I searched in the dawn only for a stray petal or two.

Ah me, what is it I find? What token left of thy love? It is no flower, no spices, no vase of perfumed water. It is thy mighty sword, flashing as a flame, heavy as a bolt of thunder. The young light of morning comes through the window and spread itself upon thy bed. The morning bird **twitters**[2] and asks, 'Woman, what hast thou got?' No, it is no flower, nor spices, nor vase of perfumed water — it is thy dreadful sword.

I sit and **muse**[3] in wonder, what gift is this of thine. I can find no place to hide it. I am ashamed to wear it, frail as I am, and it hurts me

有几个人说："瞧呀，国王的旗帜！"我们站起身来，喊道："没有时间再耽搁了！"

国王来了，——可是灯在哪儿呢？花环在哪儿呢？供国王坐的宝座又在哪儿呢？啊，丢脸！啊，把脸丢尽了！大厅在哪儿，陈设又在哪儿呢？有人说话了："叫喊也无用了！空手迎接国王，迎他到你一无所有的房间里去吧！"

打开大门，吹响海螺吧！我们黑暗凄凉之屋的国王，在深夜里降临了。雷霆在空中怒吼，黑暗随着闪电颤抖。把你破破烂烂的席子拿出来，铺在院子里吧。我们的恐怖之夜的国王，突然之间与暴风雨一同来临了。

五二

我想我应该向你要那挂在你脖子上的玫瑰花环，可是我不敢。于是我就等到早晨，在你离开的时候，从你床上去找花环的零星残余。我在黎明时分像个乞丐似的东找西寻，就为了那散落的一两片花瓣。

啊！我找到了什么呢？你的爱留下了什么信物呢？那可不是花朵，不是香料，不是一瓶香水。竟是你的一把利剑，闪闪发光如火焰，沉重如雷霆万钧。年轻的晨光从窗子里泻进来，铺在你的床上。晨鸟啁啾发问："女人，你得到了什么呢？"不，那可不是花朵，不是香料，不是一瓶香水——却是你那可怕的利剑。

我坐在那儿，心里纳罕，你这是什么信物啊？我找不到地方把它收藏起来。我这样柔弱，我不好意思佩带利剑，我把它紧抱在怀里时，它又要伤害我。然而，你

① dreary /'drɪərɪ/ a. 沉闷的，阴郁的

② twitter /'twɪtə/ v. （鸟等）吱吱叫，啁啾

③ muse /'mjuːz/ v. 沉思，冥想

when press it to my bosom. Yet shall I bear in my heart this honour of the burden of pain, this gift of thine.

From now there shall be no fear left for me in this world, and thou shalt be victorious in all my strife. Thou hast left death for my companion and I shall crown him with my life. Thy sword is with me to cut **asunder**① my bonds, and there shall be no fear left for me in the world.

From now I leave off all petty decorations. Lord of my heart, no more shall there be for me waiting and weeping in corners, no more coyness and sweetness of **demeanour**②. Thou hast given me thy sword for adornment. No more doll's decorations for me!

54

I asked nothing from thee; I uttered not my name to thine ear. When thou took'st thy leave I stood silent. I was alone by the well where the shadow of the tree fell **aslant**③, and the women had gone home with their brown earthen pitchers full to the brim. They called me and shouted, 'Come with us, the morning is wearing on to noon.' But I languidly lingered awhile lost in the midst of vague musings.

I heard not thy steps as thou camest. Thine eyes were sad when they fell on me; thy voice was tired as thou spokest low — 'Ah, I am a thirsty traveller.' I started up from my day-dreams and poured water from my jar on thy joined palms. The leaves rustled overhead; the cuckoo sang from the unseen dark, and perfume of babla flowers came from the bend of the road.

I stood speechless with shame when my name thou didst ask. Indeed, what had I done for thee to keep me in remembrance? But the

给了我这信物，这痛苦的负担，我就一定要把这荣耀铭记在心。

从今以后，我在这世界上将无所畏惧，而你亦将在我的一切斗争中获得胜利。你留下死亡和我做伴，我将以我的生命为他加冕。我带着你的剑斩断我的镣铐，我在这世界上将无所畏惧。

从今以后，我抛弃一切微不足道的装饰。我心灵的主啊，我不再在角落里等待和哭泣，也不再温柔、羞怯。你已经把你的剑给我佩带，我就不要玩偶的装饰品了。

五四

我不向你要求什么；我不向你的耳朵说出我的名字。你离去时我默默地站着。我独自留在井边，树影横斜，妇人们顶着盛满水的褐色陶罐回家去了。她们呼唤我，大声说道："同我们一起走吧，早晨正在过去，都快近中午了。"但是我仍在阑珊地流连，落入了恍惚的遐想。

你来时我没听到你的足音。你那落在我身上的眼神是悲哀的；你低低说话的声音是疲倦的。——"啊，我是个口渴的旅人。"我从我的白日梦中惊醒过来，把我罐里的水倒在你掬着的手掌里。树叶在头上簌簌地响；杜鹃在看不见的幽暗里啼鸣，从大路弯曲处传来巴勃拉花的芳香。

你问起我的名字的时候，我害羞得默默地站着。真的，我为你做了什么，竟使你念念不忘？但，我能给你饮水解渴，这点回忆将萦绕我的心头，把我的心

① asunder /əˈsʌndə/ a. 成数块的

② demeanour /dɪˈmiːnə/ n. 行为，举动

③ aslant /əˈslænt/ a. 倾斜的，歪斜的

memory that I could give water to thee to **allay**[1] thy thirst will cling to my heart and enfold it in sweetness. The morning hour is late, the bird sings in weary notes, neem leaves rustle overhead and I sit and think and think.

55

Languor is upon your heart and the slumber is still on your eyes.

Has not the word come to you that the flower is reigning in splendour among thorns? Wake, oh awaken! let not the time pass **in vain**[2]!

At the end of the stony path, in the country of virgin solitude, my friend is sitting all alone. Deceive him not. Wake, oh awaken!

What if the sky pants and trembles with the heat of the midday sun — what if the burning sand spreads its mantle of thirst —

Is there no joy in the deep of your heart? At every footfall of yours, will not the harp of the road break out in sweet music of pain?

56

Thus it is that thy joy in me is so full. Thus it is that thou hast come down to me. O thou lord of all heavens, where would be thy love if I were not?

Thou hast taken me as thy partner of all this wealth. In my heart is the endless play of thy delight. In my life thy will is ever taking shape.

And for this, thou who art the King of kings hast **decked**[3] thyself in beauty to **captivate**[4] my heart. And for this thy love loses itself in the love of thy lover, and there art thou seen in the perfect union of two.

包裹在柔情蜜意里。早晨过去了，鸟儿唱着慵倦的歌，楝树叶子在头上簌簌地响，我坐在那儿想了又想，想了又想。

五五

倦怠笼罩着你的心，你的眼睛里依旧睡意蒙眬。

难道你没有听到消息，荆棘丛中花开烂漫？醒来，啊，醒来吧！别让时光虚度！

在石径的尽头，在纯洁寂寥的乡村里，我的朋友独自坐着。别欺骗他。醒来，啊，醒来吧！

即使天空因正午的骄阳而喘息颤抖——即使灼热的砂子摊开了它干渴的表层——

难道你的内心深处就没有欢乐？难道你每走一步，大路的琴弦不会迸发出悦耳的痛苦之音吗？

五六

事情就是如此，你的欢乐是这般充满了我的身心。事情就是如此，你自天而降，来到我的身边。诸天之主啊，如果我不是你的爱人，你的爱人会在哪儿呢？

你选中我和你共享这一切财富。你的喜悦不断在我心里奏鸣音乐。你的意志永远在我的生命中化形成体。

为了这个缘故，身为万王之王的你，就打扮自己，来赢得我的心。为了这缘故，你的爱就消融在你爱人的爱里，你就以我俩合而为一的美满形象显现。

① allay /əˈleɪ/ v. 减轻,缓解

② in vain 徒然,白费力

③ deck /dek/ v. 装饰,打扮

④ captivate /ˈkæptɪveɪt/ v. 使入迷,迷惑

59

Yes, I know, this is nothing but thy love, O beloved of my heart — this golden light that dances upon the leaves, these idle clouds sailing across the sky, this passing breeze leaving its coolness upon my forehead.

The morning light has flooded my eyes — this is thy message to my heart. Thy face is bent from above, thy eyes look down on my eyes, and my heart has touched thy feet.

60

On the seashore of endless worlds children meet. The infinite sky is motionless overhead and the restless water is **boisterous**[1]. On the seashore of endless worlds the children meet with shouts and dances.

They build their houses with sand and they play with empty shells. With withered leaves they weave their boats and smilingly float them on the vast deep sea. Children have their play on the seashore of worlds.

They know not how to swim, they know not how to cast nets. Pearl fishers dive for pearls, merchants sail in their ships, while children gather pebbles and scatter them again. they seek not for hidden treasures, they know not how to cast nets.

The sea surges up with laughter and pale gleams the smile of the sea beach. Death-dealing waves sing meaningless **ballads**[2] to the children, even like a mother while rocking her baby's cradle. The sea plays with children, and pale **gleams**[3] the smile of the sea beach.

On the seashore of endless worlds children meet. **Tempest**[4] **roams**[5] in the pathless sky, ships get **wrecked**[6] in the trackless water, death is abroad and children play. On the seashore of endless worlds is the great

五九

是的，我知道，我心爱的人儿，这只是你的爱——这在叶子上跳舞的金光，这些在天空飘过的闲云，这在我的额上留下凉意的、吹过的清风。

晨光涌进我的眼睛——这是你送给我心的信息，你的脸从天下瞰，你的眼睛俯视我的眼睛，而我的心抚摸着你的双足。

六〇

孩子们在大千世界的海滨集会。头上无垠的天空是静止的，而无休止的海水奔腾澎湃。集会在大千世界的海滨，孩子们欢呼跳跃。

他们用沙子建造房屋，他们用空贝壳游戏，他们用枯叶编成小船，微笑着把小船漂浮在茫茫大海上。孩子们游戏在大千世界的海滨。

他们不会游泳，他们不会撒网。采珠人潜水寻找珍珠，商人扬帆航行，而孩子们捡来了卵石，又重新把卵石撒掉了。他们不寻求隐藏的财宝，他们不知道如何撒网。

大海欢笑着涌起洪波。海滩上闪耀着苍白的微笑。致人死命的海浪，对孩子们唱着毫无意义的歌谣，竟像母亲摇晃婴儿的摇篮一样。大海和孩子们游戏。海滩上闪耀着苍白的微笑。

孩子们在大千世界的海滨集会。风暴在无路的天空里激荡，船舶在无轨的水面上颠覆，死亡横行，但孩子们在游戏。在大千世界的海滨，孩子们正举行盛大的集会。

① boisterous /ˈbɒɪstərəs/ a. 狂暴的,猛烈的

② ballad /ˈbæləd/ n. 民歌,民谣

③ gleam /gliːm/ v. 闪烁

④ tempest /ˈtempɪst/ n. 暴风雨

⑤ roam /rəʊm/ v. 漫步,漫游

⑥ wrecked /rekt/ a. 失事船的,遇难船的

meeting of children.

62

When I bring to you coloured toys, my child, I understand why there is such a play of colours on clouds, on water, and why flowers are painted in **tints**① — when I give coloured toys to you, my child.

When I sing to make you dance I truly know why there is music in leaves, and why waves send their chorus of voices to the heart of the listening earth — when I sing to make you dance.

When I bring sweet things to your greedy hands I know why there is honey in the cup of the flowers and why fruits are secretly filled with sweet juice — when I bring sweet things to your greedy hands.

When I kiss your face to make you smile, my darling, I surely understand what pleasure streams from the sky in morning light, and what delight that is which the summer breeze brings to my body — when I kiss you to make you smile.

63

Thou hast made me known to friends whom I knew not. Thou hast given me seats in homes not my own. Thou hast brought the distant near and made a brother of the stranger.

I am uneasy at heart when I have to leave my accustomed shelter; I forget that there **abides**② the old in the new, and that there also thou abidest.

Through birth and death, in this world or in others, wherever thou leadest me it is thou, the same, the one companion of my endless life who ever linkest my heart with bonds of joy to the unfamiliar.

六二

我送你彩色玩具的时候，我的孩子，我懂得了为什么云里水里会变幻出色彩缤纷，为什么百花点染着姹紫嫣红——就在我送你彩色玩具的时候，我的孩子。

我唱着歌使你跳舞的时候，我确实明白了为什么树叶萧萧，响出音乐，为什么波浪澎湃，把合唱的歌声送到静静谛听的大地的心里——就在我唱着歌使你跳舞的时候。

我把糖果送到你贪馋的双手里的时候，我知道了为什么花蕊里有蜜，为什么水果里藏着甜汁——就在我把糖果送到你贪馋的双手里的时候。

我吻你的脸使你微笑的时候，我的宝贝，我确实领悟了晨光里从天空流下来的是什么喜悦，夏天的凉风给我的身体带来的又是什么快感——就在我吻你的脸使你微笑的时候。

六三

你使我不认识的朋友们认识了我。你在他人的家里给我安排了座位。你使疏远的变成亲近的，使陌生人成为兄弟。

我不得不离开我住惯的居所时，我的心里不安；我忘记了这是旧居迁入新居，而且你也住在那儿。

通过生和死，在这个世界或那个世界，无论你带我到哪儿，都是你，仍旧是你，我无穷生命中的唯一伴侣，永远用欢乐的链条，把我的心和不熟悉的人联系在一起。

① tint /tɪnt/ *n.* 带白的颜色，淡色

② abide /əˈbaɪd/ *v.* 居住，逗留

When one knows thee, then alien there is none, then no door is shut. Oh, grant me my prayer that I may never lose the bliss of the touch of the one in the play of many.

65

What divine drink wouldst thou have, my God, from this overflowing cup of my life?

My poet, is it thy delight to see thy creation through my eyes and to stand at the **portals**[①] of my ears silently to listen to thine own eternal harmony?

Thy world is weaving words in my mind and thy joy is adding music to them. Thou givest thyself to me in love and then feelest thine own entire sweetness in me.

66

Thou art the sky and thou art the nest as well.

O thou beautiful, there in the nest is thy love that encloses the soul with colours and sounds and odours.

There comes the morning with the golden basket in her right hand bearing the wreath of beauty, silently to crown the earth.

And there comes the evening over the lonely meadows deserted by herds, through trackless paths, carrying cool draughts of peace in her golden pitcher from the western ocean of rest.

But there, where spreads the infinite sky for the soul to take her flight in, reigns the stainless white radiance. There is no day nor night, nor form nor colour, and never, never a word.

谁一旦认识了你，谁在世上就没有陌生的人，就没有关闭的门户。啊，请允许我的祈求，让我和众人交游之际，永远不失去和你单独接触的福祉。

六五

从我那满满欲溢的生命之杯里。我的主，你想饮怎样的神圣之酒？

通过我的眼睛看你自己的创造，站在我的耳门口静听你自己的永恒的和谐乐声，我的诗人，这就是你的乐趣？

你的世界在我的心灵里织成文字，而你的欢乐又给文字配上音乐。在我们相爱时你把自己交给了我，然后又在我这儿感觉到你自己的全部温馨柔情。

六七

你是苍天，你也是巢。

啊，美丽的你，你的巢里有你的爱，这爱以色彩、声音和芳香拥抱灵魂。

清晨来了，她右手拎着金色花篮，带着美的花冠，悄悄地给大地加冕。

黄昏来了，她越过牧人都已离去的寂静牧场，穿过车马绝迹的道路，带着金色水壶来了，壶里盛着西方安息之洋清凉的和平之水。

但是，在天空无限伸展供灵魂翱翔的地方，到处是无瑕的纯白光芒。那儿无昼无夜，无形无色，而且永远、永远无言无语。

① portal /ˈpɔːtəl/ n. 门，入口

69

The same stream of life that runs through my veins night and day runs through the world and dances in rhythmic measures.

It is the same life that shoots in joy through the dust of the earth in numberless blades of grass and breaks into **tumultuous**[1] waves of leaves and flowers.

It is the same life that is rocked in the ocean-cradle of birth and of death, in **ebb**[2] and in flow.

I feel my limbs are made glorious by the touch of this world of life. And my pride is from the life-throb of ages dancing in my blood this moment.

80

I am like a remnant of a cloud of autumn uselessly roaming in the sky, O my sun ever-glorious! Thy touch has not yet melted my vapour, making me one with thy light, and thus I count months and years separated from thee.

If this be thy wish and if this be thy play, then take this fleeting emptiness of mine, paint it with colours, **gild**[3] it with gold, float it on the **wanton**[4] wind and spread it in varied wonders.

And again when it shall be thy wish to end this play at night, I shall melt and vanish away in the dark, or it may be in a smile of the white morning, in a coolness of purity transparent.

88

Deity[5] of the ruined temple! The broken strings of Vina sing no more your praise. The bells in the evening proclaim not your time of

六九

就是这在我血管里日夜奔腾的生命之流，奔腾于世界之中，按着节奏起舞。

就是这同一的生命，欢乐地从大地破土而出，化为芳草无数，发为绿叶繁花，摇曳如波浪起伏。

就是这同一的生命，随着潮汐涨落，在生与死的海洋摇篮里摇摇晃晃。

我觉得因为四肢受到这生命世界的爱抚而荣耀。而历代生命的搏动，此刻正在我的血液里舞蹈，我引以为豪。

八○

我像一片秋天的残云，徒然在空中飘荡。啊，我的永远辉煌的太阳！你的抚摩还没有化掉我的水汽，使我与你的光芒合而为一，因此，我屈指计算着同你分离的岁月。

如果这是你的愿望，如果这是你的游戏，那就抓住我这飘忽的空虚，给它染上彩色，镀上黄金，让它在放肆任性的风里飘浮，使它舒展成种种不同的奇观。

再者，如果这是你的愿望，要在夜间结束这场游戏，那我就在黑暗之中或者在白色清晨的微笑里，在透明纯净的凉意里，溶化、消失。

八八

破庙里的神明啊，七弦琴的断弦，不再弹唱赞美你的歌。晚钟也不为礼拜你而报时。你周围的空气是寂然无声的。

① tumultuous /'tjuː'mʌltjuəs/ a. 吵闹的,喧哗的

② ebb /eb/ n. 落潮,退潮

③ gild /gɪld/ v. 给…镀金
④ wanton /'wɒntən/ a. 变化无常的

⑤ deity /'diːɪtɪ/ n. 神;女神

worship. The air is still and silent about you.

In your desolate dwelling comes the **vagrant** [1] spring breeze. It brings the tidings of flowers — the flowers that for your worship are offered no more.

Your worshipper of old wanders ever longing for favour still refused. In the eventide, when fires and shadows mingle with the gloom of dust, he wearily comes back to the ruined temple with hunger in his heart.

Many a festival day comes to you in silence, deity of the ruined temple. Many a night of worship goes away with lamp unlit.

Many new images are built by masters of cunning art and carried to the holy stream of **oblivion** [2] when their time is come.

Only the deity of the ruined temple remains unworshipped in **deathless** [3] neglect.

89

No more noisy, loud words from me — such is my master's will. **Henceforth** [4] I deal in whispers. The speech of my heart will be carried on in murmurings of a song.

Men hasten to the King's market. All the buyers and sellers are there. But I have my untimely leave in the middle of the day, **in the thick of** [5] work.

Let then the flowers come out in my garden, though it is not their time; and let the midday bees strike up their lazy hum.

Full many an hour have I spent in the strife of the good and the evil, but now it is the pleasure of my playmate of the empty days to draw my heart on to him; and I know not why is this sudden call to what useless consequence!

① vagrant /'veɪgrənt/ *a.* 游移不定的,无常的

驰荡的春风吹进你凄凉的庙宇。春风带来了鲜花的消息——可不再有人以鲜花供奉给你了。

你往昔的礼拜者,徘徊又徘徊,老是渴望着仍被拒绝的恩典。黄昏来临,灯火和阴影,同朦胧暗淡的尘埃混成一片时,他怀着内心的渴望,疲倦地回到了破庙。

破庙里的神明啊,对于你,不少佳节是寂静无声到来的。不少礼拜之夜,是灯火也不点亮度过的。

技术高超的大师们造了许多新的神像,可时辰一到,就给抛弃在神圣的遗忘之河里了。

② oblivion /ə'blɪvɪən/ *n.* 遗忘

③ deathless /'deθlɪs/ *a.* 不朽的,永恒的

只有破庙里的神明,倒无人礼拜地长留在永恒的荒疏里了。

八九

我不再吵吵嚷嚷地大声谈论了——这是我的主的意旨。从此我要悄声细语。我心里的话要用低低的歌声倾诉。

④ henceforth /'hence'fɔːθ/ *ad.* 从今以后,从此以后

人们赶到国王的市场上去。所有的买主和卖主都在那儿。然而,在工作正忙的中午,我不合时宜地离开了。

尽管花期未到,还是让花儿在我园子里开放吧;让中午的蜜蜂响起懒洋洋的嗡嗡之声吧。

⑤ in the thick of 在…的最紧张时刻,在…的最激烈时

我把许多时光都花费在善与恶的斗争上了,但如今我闲暇之日的游伴,却有兴致把我的心引到他身边;我不知道何以突然召唤我走向这无谓的、无足轻重的结局!

93

I have got my leave. Bid me farewell, my brothers! I bow to you all and take my departure.

Here I give back the keys of my door — and I give up all claims to my house. I only ask for last kind words from you.

We were neighbours for long, but I received more than I could give. Now the day has dawned and the lamp that lit my dark corner is out. A summon has come and I am ready for my journey.

95

I was not aware of the moment when I first crossed the threshold of this life.

What was the power that made me open out into this vast mystery like a bud in the forest at midnight!

When in the morning I looked upon the light I felt in a moment that I was no stranger in this world, that the **inscrutable**[1] without name and form had taken me in its arms in the form of my own mother.

Even so, in death the same unknown will appear as ever known to me. And because I love this life, I know I shall love death as well.

The child cries out when from the right breast the mother takes it away, in the very next moment to find in the left one its **consolation**[2].

101

Ever in my life have I sought thee with my songs. It was they who led me from door to door, and with them have I felt about me, searching and touching my world.

It was my songs that taught me all the lessons I ever learnt; they

九三

我已经请了假。我的兄弟们，同我说声再见吧！我向你们大家鞠了躬就启程了。

我把我门上的钥匙交还——我放弃对房子的一切权利。我只是向你们要求几句最后的好话。

我们做过很久的邻居，但是我接受的多，能给予的少。如今天已破晓，照亮我黑暗角落的灯已经熄灭。召唤的命令已来，我准备启程了。

九五

我当初跨过此生的门槛之际，是不知不觉的。

是什么力量使我在这茫茫无际的神秘中开放，犹如一朵蓓蕾，深更半夜在森林里开花！

早晨我看到光明，我立刻感到我在这世界上不是个陌生人，那无名无形的不可思议者，已凭借我亲生母亲的形象，把我抱在怀里。

就是这样，在死亡之际，这同一个陌生人，将以我一向熟悉的面目出现。因为我热爱此生，我知道我将同样热爱死亡。

母亲让婴儿离开右乳的时候，婴儿就啼哭，可他转瞬之间又从左乳得到了安慰。

一〇一

我这一生将永远用诗歌来寻求你。诗歌带领我从这个门走到那个门，我和诗歌一同在我周围摸索，寻求着、接触着我的世界。

我学习的一切功课，都是诗歌教给我的；诗歌指

① inscrutable /ɪnˈskruːtəbəl/ a. 不可理解的；谜一样的

② consolation /ˌkɔnsəˈleɪʃən/ n. 安慰，慰问

showed me secret paths, they brought before my sight many a star on the horizon of my heart.

They guided me all the day long to the mysteries of the country of pleasure and pain, and, at last, to what palace gate have they brought me in the evening at the end of my journey?

点我秘密的途径，诗歌把我心里天边上的不少星星，带到了我的眼前。

诗歌整天引领我走进欢乐和痛苦的神秘境界，而最后，在我旅途终点的黄昏里，诗歌又将带我到什么宫门口呢？